HAUNTED
CHELTENHAM

HAUNTED CHELTENHAM

Diz White

The
History
Press

A gargoyle near Sudeley Castle, where ghosts linger.

Photographs in *Haunted Cheltenham* by Randall Montgomery.

First published 2010

The History Press
The Mill, Brimscombe Port
Stroud, Gloucestershire, GL5 2QG
www.thehistorypress.co.uk

ISBN 978 0 7524 5427 6
Typesetting and origination by The History Press
Printed in Great Britain

Contents

About the Author

British-born Diz White, together with her husband Randall Montgomery whose photographs illustrate this book, divides her time between a career in Hollywood, USA, as an actress and screenplay writer, and her cottage in Gloucestershire which she uses as a base for writing books about her beloved Cotswolds. In addition, she runs a DVD and mobile phone/Internet entertainment production company and can be reached through www.dizwhite.com

Other books by Diz White:

The Comedy Group Book (Smith and Kraus)
Haunted Cotswolds (The History Press)

Diz is currently putting the finishing touches on her comedic memoir about the Cotswolds, *A Love Note to the Cotswolds: Fun Adventures Buying an English Country Cottage.*

Acknowledgements

This book is dedicated to my husband Randall Montgomery, a professional photographer, who took all the photos for this book. I wish to thank him for these images, for his invaluable editing and computer expertise and most of all for his incredible patience and hard work as he lovingly helped me put this book together. I also dedicate this book to my mother Josephine Ashley, the poet, and to my dear family.

I also wish to thank Monica B. Morris, author of *Goodnight Children, Everywhere: Voices of Evacuees* (The History Press) for her help, encouragement and superb editing skills.

This book would not have been possible without the vision of my commissioning editor, Nicola Guy. I wish to convey my thanks to her and her excellent team at The History Press.

Another thank you is gratefully given to all the helpful inhabitants of Cheltenham, perhaps the most elegant town in England, who told me their spooky stories and shared their ghostly haunts.

Introduction

Ch…Ch…Ch…Cheltenham. That is how the frightened folks who come from this charming town pronounce its name as their teeth chatter in chilled horror after an encounter with any of its numerous spectres.

The town itself has its fair share of ghouls, shades and poltergeists, but also within the borough lies Prestbury, said to be the most haunted village in the entire United Kingdom. Here there are so many visitors from the other side that anyone who walks down its main street is liable to be left gibbering, shivering and drooling with fear in addition to becoming pop-eyed with disbelief; the ghosts in this village are said to be so plentiful that they not only turn anyone who lays eyes on them into blubbering wrecks, but actually scare the wits out of each other.

One poor fellow who braved a walk through Prestbury churchyard at night was even scared out of his clothes. After an encounter with the notorious spectre of the Black Abbot of Prestbury, he was left shaking so badly that his loosely held jogging trousers ended up around his ankles. It takes a really good haunting to do that.

Apparently Prestbury is as crowded as the London Underground at rush hour, with ghouls bumping into their fellow shades so frequently that they end up, on occasion, walking right through one another.

The rich history of this region has surely helped supply it with the abundance of spooks, shades, phantoms, wraiths, banshees, goblins, sprites, hobgoblins, ghouls, glowing orbs, spectres, shape-shifters, ley line manifestations and poltergeists. The ghosts who haunt Cheltenham and its surrounds are indeed a creepy crowd. In the true-life stories that follow, there are tales of headless horsemen, marauding monks, Civil War spooks, grotto ghouls, terrified terrier dogs, phantom funerals, strangling shades, weeping widows, pub poltergeists, time-stealing sprites, haunted housekeepers, a peeping Thomasina, phantom shepherds, spinet-playing shades and a bedroom-wrecking banshee.

Cheltenham lies in the centre of the Cotswolds and with its Georgian and Regency architecture and its position in the shadow of the limestone escarpment of Cleeve Hill, which provides stunning views, it is a picture-perfect example of an unspoiled Cotswold town.

The Romans were perhaps the first settlers to supply the Cheltenham area with a sample of its ghost contingent. The murder and mayhem they brought with them during their occupation of Britain must have led to many a lost soul wandering through the realm of the undead. The ruins of a Roman villa were discovered in the Withington area, on the outskirts of Cheltenham, when a mosaic floor and part of a hypercaust (underfloor heating system) were found. These and other findings near Cheltenham, together with much evidence of Roman occupation in nearby Chedworth and Cirencester, show that the local inhabitants must have been completely subjugated by their conquerors. It is well documented that these poor inhabitants endured hideous torture at the hands of their Roman invaders before they were turned into slaves.

After the decline of the Roman Empire, much of Britain returned to its former low-key level of barbarism as various tribes struggled for power with intermittent bloody battles being fought by various Saxon and Mercian kings. Next, the Norman Conquest decimated the population of Britain, with its own contribution of blood and gore.

But it was the English Civil War that really impinged on this area, with numerous skirmishes played out in and around Cheltenham, particularly in Prestbury. Many sightings of Roundhead and Cavalier apparitions have contributed to the ghost stories of the area and the horrors of this war must have increased the ghost population markedly.

Following the Dissolution of the Monasteries by Henry VIII in 1539, religious persecution was rife. In that era priests were hunted down like dogs and many priest holes have been discovered in the Cheltenham area, especially in chimneys and attics, where these desperate men hid from their enemies. Torture and execution was often the fate of these priests when they were caught and their restless souls are the subject of many a spine-chilling ghost story.

The Normans brought their masonry expertise along with them when they invaded Britain and these skills gave the Cotswolds its distinctive appearance. These same skills were handed down through the centuries and helped make Cheltenham the elegant town it is today.

Wool production, which greatly contributed to the wealth of the area during medieval times, initially began before the Roman occupation, literally as a cottage industry, and ramped up in volume over the next few hundred years. Streams and rivers from the hills of the Cotswolds provided the energy to power the mills and by the fifteenth century the whole area was very much dependent on its wool output.

The Costwold area acquired its name from the sheep enclosures, or 'cots', combined with the description of the hills which during past times were known as 'wolds'. The poor quality of land in this area was found to be unsuitable for arable farming but was ideal for the raising of sheep.

By the 1800s, however, the Cotswolds' dominance of the wool market began to fall away as other producers rose up. With no funds for development the area remained stagnant,

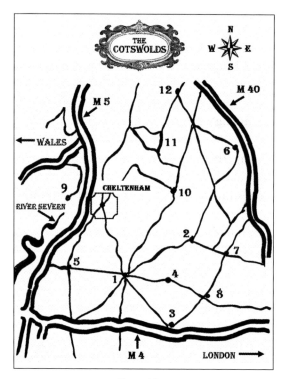

leading to the current 'frozen in time' appearance of many of its towns and villages. The result of this decline was, in fact, a good one for the architectural aspects of the area. As a result of it the Cotswolds was not subsequently subjected to the heavy handedness of Victorian architectural styles which are evident in the disastrous make-over of architectural gems in other areas. This gorgeous region, with its rolling hills, breathtaking vistas, seventeenth-century cottages, sumptuous wool churches, picturesque drystone walls and elegant town and manor houses, is idyllic on a perfect summer day but can turn hair-raisingly creepy after the sun goes down.

Close to Cheltenham lies the Belas Knap long barrow burial mound, a recommended place for the courageous, thrill-seeking ghost hunter to explore, for the long-dead souls from its Neolithic past are said to lure the unwary visitor into its haunted chambers with sometimes tragic results.

Cheltenham is said to be one of the most elegant towns in the Cotswolds and it certainly lives up to that description, sporting magnificent Regency buildings laid out in the form of terraces, squares and crescents complete with beautifully designed parks and gardens. Many of these buildings are grouped around the perfectly proportioned tree-lined Promenade, with its top-of-the-line shops and classically constructed buildings.

Cheltenham is a lively town and offers many interesting activities and fascinating features to explore, including the Montpellier Assembly Rooms, Imperial Gardens, Pittville Pump Room, Cheltenham Racecourse, St Mary's Church, Royal Crescent, the John Dower Building, the Neptune Fountain, the Promenade and the Gustav Holst Museum, to name but a few.

Cheltenham's fortunes improved after its modest beginnings with the discovery in 1715 of a small spring that contained salt crystals. This spring was turned into the first pump room in the town. A few years later the original owner's son-in-law, Henry Skillicorne, erected a substantial building around this spring and called it a 'spa'.

John Forbes the architect was commissioned by Joseph Pitt to build a pump room in the Palladian style. Forbes completed a magnificently proportioned building based on Greek architecture using Ionic columns that incorporated a design copied from a temple lying on the banks of the River Ilissus near Athens.

The entire front of the spa is colonnaded and two corners of the building are decorated with monolithic figures of Aesculapius, Hygia and Hippocrates. The newly named Pittville Pump Room, with its canted windows and graceful dome featuring coffering with rosettes, along with the spa, is a perfect example of Regency elegance. A grand ball was attended by leading society figures to celebrate the opening of the spa on 20 July 1830. A visit to the spa to take the waters was only a small part of the attractions on offer at the Pittville Pump Room, as many other events were also included. Gala fêtes, firework displays, band recitals and opportunities to 'promenade' around the flower-filled grounds were also part of the fun. Later, Pitt ran into money difficulties but his loss was Cheltenham's gain for he sold the pump room to the borough for £5,400 in 1890.

The pump room fell into disrepair after being requisitioned for use during the Second World War and was subsequently in danger of collapse. Eventually it was rescued and renovated, paid for by public subscription. After partial restoration the pump room was reopened in 1960 by the Duke of Wellington. Today, this room is used on most days of the year for public and private functions and is also a very popular wedding venue.

The Pittville Pump Room is located in Pittville Park, two miles from the centre of town, and the spa waters are still taken after being pumped from an 80ft well up to a fountain in the foyer. This water is said to be the only natural alkaline water in Great Britain.

In the nineteenth century many Army officers, administrators and retirees from careers abroad settled here to cure any ailments caught in the tropics.

Pittville Pump Room, Cheltenham.

It was during the first thirty or forty years of the nineteenth century that a good part of Cheltenham was constructed using the Regency architectural style that so distinguishes it to this day. This style, which owed much of its distinctive appearance to the Georgian architecture from earlier times, began its rise to prominence when George IV was Prince Regent and further construction followed a similar design. Regency houses were classical in design and made great use of fluted quasi-Greek columns, moulded cornices and pediment architraves. These houses, often arranged in terraces, were also characterised by tall, narrow windows, balconies of intricately patterned, delicate, wrought iron and exquisitely proportioned exteriors which were finished without excessive decorative additions.

Some say that a peculiar phenomena, namely ley lines, has contributed to the harmonious architectural design of Cheltenham. Many of these ley lines run through the region and intersect in a particular way, creating electromagnetic fields that can be beneficial or, alternatively, can cause ghostly spiritual disturbances. These ley lines are thought to link up ancient buildings of spiritual and religious significance in a straight line, some measuring hundreds of miles, and were first observed in the early eighteenth century.

Ley lines are thought to be of particular significance in Prestbury and link directly to Llanthony Priory in Wales. This may account for the many hauntings of St Mary's

Church by the Black Abbot of Prestbury, who was a member of one of the cells of this priory.

Any ghost hunters who visit Prestbury might, after they have spent significant time there, want to suggest to their hosts the following formula for laying a spectre. This recipe appears in J. A. Brook's *Ghosts and Witches of the Cotswolds*. This technique requires gathering together, among other things, a barrel of spirits and a dozen clergymen (difficulties may arise in convincing the clergymen to take part), and then performing a ceremony. This ceremony would presumably take the form of an exorcism similar to the medieval bell, book and candle ritual. Next, a master carpenter and a bricklayer must be hired to seal off the doors and the windows of the room in which the haunting took place. No trace of the room's existence should be in evidence at the end of the construction work. Apparently this technique works and a number of these 'vanished' rooms have been discovered in period houses. Perhaps this ghost-laying formula will prove a little difficult to accomplish, but when the ghosts are out in force it is good to have a failsafe resource on which to fall back.

Prestbury is close to what is now known as Cheltenham Racecourse, and that too has a connection with a ghost. This racecourse is world famous and is often visited by royalty. It was a favourite of the Queen Mother in her day, and is particularly renowned for its National Hunt Festival and Gold Cup race held every March.

Lord Ellenborough first offered his land for racing in 1831 after gambling and racing were criticised by the Revd Francis Close. Cheltenham Racecourse has been in operation as a racing venue since 1902 and now consists of two racecourses, appropriately named the Old and the New. Both courses sport many well-designed fences which test the jockey's jumping ability to the utmost.

The grandstand, which is located below the escarpment of Cleeve Hill, affords majestic views of the racing and was opened by the Queen Mother in 1979. The reopened Gloucestershire-Warwickshire Railway runs a steam train that brings race-goers directly to the course. The *King George* became the first steam locomotive to travel to the racecourse and for over thirty years allowed attendees to arrive 'by rail at the races'. HRH the Princess Royal reopened Cheltenham Racecourse railway station in 2003.

Perhaps the greatest jockey ever, Fred Archer, was born in Cheltenham. He was the son of William Archer, who was the winner of the Grand National on Little Charlie in 1858. William also once owned the King's Arms public house in Prestbury. Fred Archer was apprenticed as an eleven-year-old boy to the trainer Mathew Dawson. In 1872 he won the Cesarewitch, his first Classic race, and subsequently in 1884, after he won the 2,000 Guineas, went to work for Lord Falmouth as a retained jockey. He married Mathew Dawson's niece, Helen Rose, in 1884.

Archer won 2,748 races including twenty-one Classics. But, in the end, his was a tragic story. Although he was a natural horseman his height, 5ft 10in, worked against him, making it hard for him to maintain the low weight required to qualify for riding.

Cheltenham Racecourse.

Fred Archer's father owned this pub in Prestbury.

His wins turned him into a living legend and some women were known to faint at the sight of him. Despite his great success he took his own life at the age of twenty-nine. He had been despondent over the death of his wife in childbirth two years previously and some say that this, combined with the drastic measures he took to ride at the prescribed weight, sent him into a delirium during which he shot himself. Others say that the delirium that caused him to take his own life was brought on by an attack of typhus.

The National Horseracing Museum exhibits a selection of Fred Archer's memorabilia and his ghost is said to haunt Newmarket Racecourse, the scene of so many of his triumphs. His shade has been seen riding across the course on a light grey horse on a number of occasions.

In this book the Cheltenham Ghost, in addition to a plethora of other ghosts in this elegant town, the myriad Prestbury poltergeists and a handful of shades from surrounding areas, make up a splendid selection of scary stories for the enjoyment of every ghost reader.

Dip into these tales at any time or wait for a night when the wind whistles through the trees and then turn the lights down low, gather a group of ghost lovers together and take turns reading this book out loud from cover to cover. Afterwards no talking should be attempted until everybody's teeth stop chattering, for there's nothing creepier that haunted Ch...Ch...Cheltenham.

Victorian painting of Fred Archer, the jockey.

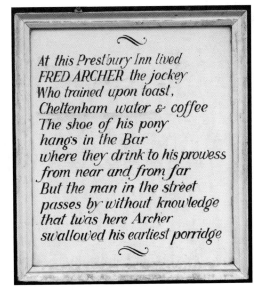

At this Prestbury Inn lived
FRED ARCHER the jockey
Who trained upon toast,
Cheltenham water & coffee
The shoe of his pony
hangs in the Bar
where they drink to his prowess
from near and from far
But the man in the street
passes by without knowledge
that twas here Archer
swallowed his earliest porridge

A sign about Fred Archer, the jockey whose ghost haunts Newmarket.

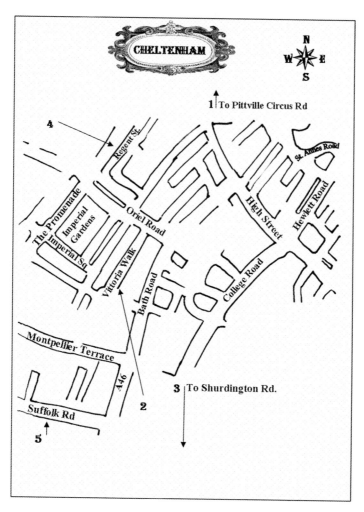

Key to Map

Story	Location	Story Title
1	Pittville Circus Road	The Cheltenham Ghost
2	Vittoria Walk	The Ghosts of Vittoria Walk
3	Shurdington Road	The Undead Drinker
4	Regent Street	The Eerie Everyman Theatre
5	Suffolk Road	The Suffolk Arms Poltergeist

The numbers on the maps in this book of Cheltenham, Prestbury and Cheltenham's environs refer to the locations of the stories throughout the book. The number at the beginning of each story enables the reader to easily find the location of the story on the map at the beginning of each chapter.

one

Cheltenham

1 The Cheltenham Ghost

The Cheltenham Ghost, or the Morton Case as it is sometimes called, is of sufficient interest and stretches over such a long period of time that it warrants a full telling of the entire case. The Cheltenham Ghost story is divided into three segments.

When the Society for Psychical Research first investigated this case in the late nineteenth century it was thought best not to reveal the identity of the family whose home had been haunted, and also not to disclose the name of the person whose shade was suspected of causing the haunting. The pseudonym Morton was used to refer to this case until B. Adby Collins' book *The Morton Ghost* was published. Since that time the true names of those involved in this chilling story have been revealed and are used in this chapter.

The Ghoul of Garden Reach

Rose saw the ghost first. It was the middle of June and very hot. It was so hot that the air became distorted and seemed to shimmer as it bounced off walls and windows. Rose blinked. She had a headache and thought her mind was playing tricks on her. Surely that was the reason she was staring at an absolute stranger who had suddenly appeared in the drawing room. This stranger had not been there a second before. Rose blinked several more times, but the woman was still there, standing by the sofa. Rose was puzzled. Someone was in her home and appeared to be absolutely real. However, no noise had been made to announce this person's arrival. This was odd as the door to the drawing room had a squeaking hinge and, what is more, it was the only entrance into the room.

Rose was about to open her mouth to say something when this same door opened behind her, with its customary screech of metal on metal, and the parlour maid entered with a tea tray. Rose watched the maid's face to see if she noticed anything amiss. Just at that moment the stranger moved. Rose and the maid stared in horror as this apparition walked right through a table. The tea tray was dropped with a crash and an accompanying scream.

Now Rose was scared. Her first impulse was to run to the upstairs bedroom where her invalid mother lay sleeping, but she stopped herself. Her mother was ill enough and this could make things worse. She wished her father was at home so that she could go running to him and have him make everything all right, as he did when she was a child. Her father was Captain Despard and he had moved his family into this large house on Pittville Circus Road, which he had renamed 'Garden Reach', only two months before in April 1882.

The house had stood empty for a long time before the family took it and there were reports of it being haunted. A note of warning had gone unheeded by the Despard family when the house had been offered for rent at half the normal rate for a building of this size. The family had dismissed rumours of the house being haunted and had been very happy to move into it. Every member of the family maintained that ghosts did not exist.

Rose dashed for the door leaving the maid quivering, shaking and unable to move. She stifled her screams as she fled into the drawing room to find her brother and, between fits of hysterical sobbing, described the ghost to him. Initially, she had been sure that this stranger was a real person so she had looked at her closely before realising that she was a ghoul. By now the maid had recovered enough to verify all that had happened.

Rose described seeing a tall woman of thirty-five or forty years of age. This woman was dressed in widow's weeds – typical Victorian mourning dress. She was wearing a black, floor-length dress made of bombazine with many petticoats, a cashmere shawl trimmed in black ostrich feathers, long black gloves, high-buttoned black boots and jet jewellery. Her black hat had a veil fastened to it which was pulled back. Her hair was in a neat bun and she partially obscured her face by holding a black-edged handkerchief close to it, making it hard for Rose to properly see her features.

When Captain Despard heard his daughter's story he called in an expert to investigate this frightening manifestation. The expert was Frederick W.H. Myers. At that time there was a great upsurge of interest in spiritualism and as a result mediums were frequently employed to conduct séances. Unfortunately, the unsuspecting public were plagued by shysters, frauds and cranks who posed as experts adept at getting in touch with those from the other side. These predators exploited the bereaved's desperate attempts to make contact with their departed loved ones, prompting a call for something to be done about it.

Frederick William Henry Myers was an early ghost hunter whose investigations led him to Cheltenham after he co-founded the Society of Psychical Research (SPR) in Cambridge in the late nineteenth century.

The society's purpose was (and still is) to establish the truth about psychic or paranormal phenomena and when it was first formed telepathy, mesmerism, mediums, apparitions and séances were researched. When first formed, the society stated that its aimed to investigate 'events and abilities commonly described as psychic or paranormal by promoting and supporting important research in this area'. The society conducted some of the first systematic investigations of paranormal phenomena ever carried out.

Formed by a band of like-minded thinkers including Myers, William Fletcher Barrett, Henry Sidgwick, Edmund Dawson Rogers and Edmund Gurney, the SPR eventually set up its headquarters in Marloes Road, London. The society publishes the magazine *Paranormal Review* and the *Society for Psychical Research Journal* (JSPR). Today the organisation is divided between its London headquarters and Cambridge where its archives are stored.

Frederick W.H. Myers and his cohorts were joined in their search for the truth about paranormal phenomena by another like-minded debunker of the fakes and frauds pervading this field. This was Harry Price, who was to become a key figure in the ghost hunting movement of the time. Investigators called in to help in this endeavour were drawn from esteemed professions in order to give credence to the integrity of the work. Members of the scientific establishment, psychologists and doctors all took a hand in trying to sort out genuine manifestations from those stage-managed by tricksters.

During Harry Price's investigations a medium named Helen Duncan was paid £50 to be examined under scientific conditions; the ectoplasm she claimed to produce turned out to be egg white. In 1935 Harry Price also carried out research into Karachi's Indian Rope Trick and Kuda Bux's fire-walking abilities. He went on to write *Confessions of a Ghost Hunter,* which was published in 1936, and *Poltergeist Over England*, published in 1945.

Frederick Myers studied the strange phenomena that took place in Garden Reach for over four years. He traced the history of the building, which had been bought brand new in 1860 by one Henry Swinhoe, a retired Army surgeon. At this time the rambling Victorian house, with its three stories, narrow windows and tall chimneys, was named St Anne's.

After only two years of happily living in the house Swinhoe's beloved wife died, her death driving him to drink to ease the pain of his loss. After a period of time he remarried, to a woman named Imogen, who proved to be something of a shrew. She thought she could reform her new husband and put a stop to his drinking, but it was not to be. Swinhoe had hidden his first wife's jewellery under the floor of the house to keep the hoard safe and eventually leave a legacy for his children. Imogen wanted the jewels but her husband refused to give them up, and this caused endless fights between the two. Swinhoe died in 1876 and Imogen, succumbing to alcoholism in her own unhappiness, followed him barely two years later.

Frederick Myers finally surmised that it was Swindhoe's first wife who was haunting the house. The ghost of this woman who had forced the Despard's maid to drop the tea tray made frequent appearances subsequently, and eventually the Despard's daughter,

Ghosts roam this house, once known as Garden Reach.

Rose, lost her fear and was able to speak to this apparition when it appeared. Rose kept a written account of her every encounter with the ghost, along with those of the staff and her siblings. Neither Captain Despard nor his invalid wife ever reported that the ghost made an appearance to them. Rose sent her account to a friend, Catherine Campbell, living in the north of England, and Frederick Myers consulted the Campbell account during his investigation. Following this, Myers wrote a detailed description of the hauntings in Volume VIII of the *Proceedings of the Society for Psychical Research*, changing the family name to Morton and obscuring the location of the house. For many years these events were known as the Morton Case or the Cheltenham Ghost.

One rumour of the time claims that this ghost was, in fact, not a ghost at all but the mistress of Captain Despard. When this woman was spotted by members of the family or the staff she was passed off by him as 'a ghost'. This theory does fit with one account of Rose's first meeting with the ghost (or in this case Despard's mistress) that differs from the one described above. In this account Rose heard someone in the passage outside her bedroom late at night. She picked up a lighted candle and opened her door to investigate. She saw a tall lady dressed in black hovering at the top of the stairs. Just as Rose moved forward to better see this figure her candle flickered out. In this account, Rose reacted as if the person she saw was not a ghost, so perhaps there is something to this theory.

Subsequently, there were so many witnesses to the visits of this ghostly lady that a genuine manifestation could not be discounted.

Rose tried various ways of communicating with this sad apparition and at one time the ghost opened her mouth to answer one of the questions put to her, but the only sound heard was a strangled gasp. This apparition, always wearing her widow's weeds, would walk down the stairs and enter either the anteroom or the drawing room and stand by the sofa. At first, other members of the family mistook her for a real person, just as Rose had. The apparition would wander around the sofa, sometimes walking through furniture, still with her black-edged handkerchief held to her face, weeping softly. Sometimes she was found seated at a writing desk, while at other times she would sit next to one of Rose's sisters while she was playing the piano, as if waiting to turn a page of music. Eventually she would walk back to the hallway and disappear down it, making her way towards the garden. Once, when several of Rose's six brother and sisters were in the garden, they saw the widow's ghost walking through it, sadly weeping as before.

Only certain members of the family could actually see the apparition, but those who reported a sighting remarked on the solidity of this ghost. There was nothing insubstantial or transparent about her. In all, almost two dozen members of the family and staff were actually able to see this spectre, but everybody in the household heard her footsteps, especially on the stairs. Sometimes they were accompanied a second set of footsteps. These were leaden and plodding, like those of a heavyset man. On other occasions these footsteps were heard along with bumps, clanking, thuds and rattling chains.

The entire family tried various ways of trapping the ghost. They would lie in wait, sometimes for hours, for her to appear. On a number of occasions a thread was tied across doorways or the stairs but the ghost simply passed right through, leaving them undisturbed.

Rose also tried to touch the ghost but every time she did the spirit moved just out of her reach. If the ghost was cornered by several members of the family she simply disappeared.

Finally, in 1886, the ghost gradually began fading away, but not before Rose had gathered her siblings and servants together to form a circle around this sad restless spirit when she appeared one day. The family tried to entrap her but as everybody closed in she slipped between two of Rose's sisters' tightly clutched hands and completely disappeared.

The Terrified Terrier of Garden Reach

As mentioned in the last segment, the apparition of Garden Reach was thought to be the wife of the first owner of this residence – a Mrs Swinhoe. When her spirit appeared before the Despard family it is said that she particularly scared the family dog, which was, according to Frederick Myers, a small terrier. This dog would have pre-recognition of the ghost, especially as she was about to glide down from the upper storey. In advance of a visitation the terrier would leave its usual sleeping spot on the back porch and wait at the bottom of the stairs, anxiously wagging its tail and running in circles. On a number of occasions the dog heralded the ghost's appearances by two or three minutes in advance. As the spirit descended the stairs and moved around the room, the dog would follow her or circle around her as if she were made of flesh and blood.

Psychic abilities in animals have long been investigated and found, in many cases, to be extraordinarily acute. The technical term for this ability, 'anpsi', was coined by J.B. Rhine. Animals seem to be able to sense approaching danger long before humans can. Service dogs, particularly those owned by people with severe medical challenges, save lives on a daily basis using these skills; in the case of epileptics, these dogs have a way of anticipating the coming seizure and are able to give ample advance warning. Animals can also predict natural disasters such as earthquakes or hurricanes and usually flee the area before danger hits. Pre-recognition in animals is often seen when a dog will, in advance of the arrival of its owner, run to the front door to greet him or her even though that time may vary day by day.

J.B. Rhine's investigations into the psychic abilities of animals came out of his initial studies into parapsychology. Rhine was born in 1895 in Pennsylvania and started his career as a botanist. One day he attended a lecture by Sir Arthur Conan Doyle, who was claiming scientific proof of communications with those on the other side. This inspired Rhine to completely change course. He conducted a series of controlled experiments while working at the laboratory of Duke University in Durham, North Carolina, to prove that this communication was possible. In collaboration with Professor William McDougall, chairman of the Department of Psychology, Rhine created the term 'extrasensory perception' (ESP) to describe the ability of certain people who were able to acquire information without the use of the five senses. He used the word 'parapsychology' to distinguish his study from mainstream psychology.

Rhine was the first to apply scientific methodology to this study, utilising double-blind experiments in parapsychology, psychokinesis (the power to influence events by non-physical means, e.g. controlling the roll of dice), and precognition (the ability to foretell events and telepathy). He founded the Parapsychological Association and published his book *Extrasensory Perception* in 1934.

Rhine's investigations into poltergeist activity and their connections with psychokinetic abilities were interesting. His experiments showed that approximately a quarter of the cases investigated had no logical explanation. He was also in touch with the Revd Luther Shultz, and it was Shultz who had initial contact with the 1949 case of the possessed boy who became the subject of the book and feature film *The Exorcist*. The Revd Shultz was of the opinion that a poltergeist, and not possession by the Devil, was the cause of this boy's experience.

J.B. Rhine conducted many experiments in animal precognition before he died in 1980, and afterwards his work in this area was carried on by his daughter, Sally Rhine Feather.

Ghostly Garden Reach is situated on this street in Cheltenham.

It is easy to see why this team of father and daughter scientists would have been interested in the family dog at Garden Reach, as they had probably already heard reports of 'the black dogs of Gloucestershire'. These canine spectres have been well documented as they have often haunted this county, especially the churchyards and country lanes, usually in packs. The most infamous of these dogs is Black Shuck. This spectre is known for his shape-shifting abilities and has frequently been seen changing into horrific monsters, sometimes spitting fire and drooling blood. On other occasions this dog has turned into a ghastly old crone with sharp pointed teeth or a Mephistophelian figure who tries to tear the eyes out of anyone who observes him. During the Middle Ages herdsmen would identify the spot where a black dog apparition had been seen and then cover up the eyes of their animals as they passed by in order to prevent any interaction with these terrible beasts.

The small terrier of Garden Reach seemed to react to some communication it received from Mrs Swinhoe's apparition, although the family members who witnessed this interaction heard no sound. There must have been some communication taking place between this entity and the dog – perhaps a telepathic message – as it was reported that a typical exchange led to the poor animal suddenly turning wide-eyed, becoming seized with terror, shaking violently and slinking away, yelping pitifully with his tail between his legs.

The Garden Reach Ghoul Returns

However, the ghoul of Garden Reach returned long after the Despards has left, and light footsteps could still be heard from her until 1892. A later owner of the house reported seeing this same ghost in the front garden of the house many times in the early 1900s. Much later, Garden Reach was converted into a private school but the owners were forced to close it down due to 'persistent disturbances caused by paranormal phenomena'. These phenomena were not specified.

Garden Reach was eventually turned into a block of flats and there is a confirmed report of a Mr Thorn, a tenant, being haunted by a ghost between 1957-1962. During this time Mr Thorn allowed a relative to borrow his flat. This hapless relation was subjected to an incredibly violent manifestation on one dark and stormy winter night.

It all began when this relative was awoken in the middle of the night after experiencing a sharp slap to his face. He was so shocked that he began shaking violently and when he fumbled for his spectacles he inadvertently knocked over his bedside lamp and smashed it. During this the spectacles were lost. Next, he felt as if he were being strangled as a sustained pressure was applied to his windpipe. It was only when he managed to gasp a few words of a prayer, between strangled choking, that the pressure on his throat suddenly ceased. Still in the pitch dark, he cowered in fear as an evil force took possession of the bedroom and literally ripped it apart. He was almost killed when a heavy wardrobe tipped over and crashed into the bed frame, missing him by inches and sending shards of splintered wood shooting around the room like jagged arrows. After this the bed was upended with Mr Thorn's relative still in it, though by now he had burrowed under the bedcovers as he quivered in fear. Next, the bedroom door was torn off its hinges and hurled across the room. Shortly thereafter, a heavy chair flew through the air and smashed a large mirror into a thousand splinters. Finally, a hand-wash basin was ripped from the wall and waves of icy water immediately cascaded through the room from the broken plumbing.

Mr Thorn's relative was speechless with terror and only escaped by feeling his way blindly along a wall until he found the broken doorframe and slipped through. He later stated that he felt he managed to get free only because this terrible, evil force was occupied with ripping the ceiling light fixture from its fitting amid sparking electricity that immediately started a fire. Needless to say this poor, battered fellow never returned to the block of flats that was once Garden Reach.

2 The Ghosts of Vittoria Walk

One of England's greatest novelists, Thomas Hardy, lived for a time in a house in Vittoria Walk. This author and poet was made famous by such classics as *Tess of the D'Urbervilles, Jude the Obscure, The Dynasts* and *The Mayor of Casterbridge*. Several of these books have become the subject of films and other dramatisations.

Hardy was born on 2 June 1840 in a cottage in Higher Brockhampton, Dorset. Despite his success as a novelist his greatest ambition was to be remembered as a poet. However, even though he wrote over 1,000 poems, the fourteen novels he authored gave him far greater recognition.

Hardy's father was a master mason and builder, and his son followed in his footsteps, initially becoming an architect. However, Hardy gradually realised his talents lay elsewhere and began writing novels. He continued his career in architecture until his writing became so successful that he could devote his energies to writing full-time.

He married Emma Lavinia Gifford in 1874 and the two set up home in London, but before long returned to live in Dorset. After a number of years they drifted apart and separated. However, after his wife's death Hardy seemed to have suffered guilt at the loss of their relationship and some of his best poems came out of his remorse over her death. In 1885 Hardy moved to Max Gate in Dorset, the home he built and lived in for over forty years. He enlarged it after the success of his novel *Jude the Obscure* and it is now a National Trust property. Hardy died on 11 January 1928 and his heart was buried in the parish churchyard at Stinsford in Dorset, close to the grave of his parents.

The house in Cheltenham in which Hardy lived was apparently populated by many ghosts whose activities created numerous manifestations. These disturbances often took the form of floating ectoplasm, which would sometimes take the shape of a human face. This wraith-like image of a man's visage usually floated up towards the ceiling before fading from view. The ectoplasm would, on other occasions, wrap itself around those who witnessed its appearance. Freezing cold and scalding hot temperature changes always accompanied the ectoplasm when it materialised. It is not known, however, whether these spirits were connected with Hardy or his wife.

3 The Undead Drinker

The Leckhampton Inn at 33 Shurdington Road, once a jolly local pub, was the site of an eerie haunting in 1997. The landlord was busy serving customers as usual when a man came into the pub with his dog and stood at the bar. 'What will you have sir?' asked the landlord. This man did not answer, and the landlord turned away to reach for his cloth in order to wipe down the bar. He turned back expecting his customer to have made up his mind but in that split second this man and his dog had disappeared.

There is no way this mysterious man could have reached the door or any other part of the bar in the time it took the landlord to reach for his cloth. The landlord was so astonished that he asked everyone in the bar what had happened. It turned out that another customer had known of this mysterious man and his dog when both had made an earlier appearance. The landlord was shown a picture of an old customer who had always stood at that very same spot at the bar and he recognised him immediately. The landlord felt that some kind of magic trick had been used and wanted to know where he could reach this customer to ask how it had been done. His face turned pale and he had to sit down when told that this man had died a number of years before.

4 The Eerie Everyman Theatre

The figure moved slightly and then suddenly became transparent. The stagehand rubbed his eyes. He had been working very long hours preparing for the opening night of a new play at the Everyman Theatre and as it was 3 a.m. he was very tired. He was alone, or so he thought, as all his colleagues had departed the theatre earlier leaving him to finish off some urgent tasks. What could a woman dressed in Edwardian clothing possibly be doing in the theatre at this hour? He thought he must have been hallucinating from lack of sleep. He had been securing some stage scenery when something moved in the balcony of the upper circle. When he looked again nothing had changed – the figure was still there and she was still transparent. He blinked and rubbed his eyes and looked again. This shadowy figure glided a few feet up one of the aisles and then promptly disappeared.

The Everyman Theatre, which is in the centre of Cheltenham and can be reached through the Regent Arcade or the main entrance on Regent Street, was originally designed by Frank Matcham, thought to be one of the greatest architects of his time. Here, one of Matcham's finest theatre interiors survives to this day largely intact,

The haunted Everyman Theatre in Cheltenham.

featuring a semi-circular proscenium arch with a safety curtain painted in the *trompe l'oeil* style depicting lush velvet drapes and cherubic figures. The intimate auditorium is framed by white-painted balconies decorated with moulded plasterwork foliage and dominated by a magnificent Adam-style plasterwork ceiling. The updated exterior of the theatre is primarily of cheery, red brickwork with circular windows in the upper stories and an elegant glassed-in colonnade decorated with wrought iron tracery.

The theatre was immediately successful when it first opened in 1891 under its original name of the New Theatre and Opera House. A triumphant performance by Lily Langtry launched a sold-out season and many other big-name stars went on to grace its stage with their performances, including Ellen Terry, H.B. Irving, Charlie Chaplin, Fred Karno and Sir John Gielgud.

It is thought that the apparition in Edwardian dress who haunted the upper balcony could have been the shade of Lily Langtry, the first performer at the theatre.

Lily Langtry, a well-known actress of her day, was possibly more famous for her affairs with prominent men than for her stage acting. This vivacious woman was born in 1853 in Jersey, the daughter of the Revd William Corbet Le Breton, and in 1874 married prosperous Irish landowner Edward Langtry primarily, it is said, because he possessed a yacht. Her portrait was painted by Millais and displayed at the Royal Academy in London. The painting shows the actress holding a lily in her hand and this image helped create her soubriquet, the 'Jersey Lily'. She was much sought-after for her beauty and wit and was the first woman to popularise the wearing of 'the little black dress', a wardrobe necessity that has remained such a ubiquitous fashion staple among elegant women to this day.

Albert Edward (Bertie), the philandering Prince of Wales who was later to become Edward VII, arranged to be seated next to Lily Langtry during a dinner party in 1877. He had heard tales of Lily's vivid personality and proceeded to proposition her while her husband looked on from the other end of the table. She became the Prince of Wales' mistress and the affair lasted until June 1880.

When the affair with Bertie ended Lily lost much of the royal patronage that went with it, and as she was living above her means her debts quickly piled up. Bankruptcy followed, but Lily seemed undeterred and continued to have affairs with several prominent men. When she gave birth to a daughter, the baby's paternity was in doubt as Lily was conducting several liaisons at the time. Prince Louie of Battenburg was touted as the father but he vehemently denied the possibility. However, his son Dickie Mountbatten, Earl of Burma, firmly believed that this baby, named Jeanne Marie, was sired by his father.

Oscar Wilde suggested that Lily Langtry begin a stage career and her first performance was in *She Stoops to Conquer* in the Haymarket Theatre, London. Later, this production toured the United States to great success. Lily went on to conquer the theatre-going public and several more prominent men, including a trio of American

A ghost appeared on the second balcony of the Everyman.

millionaires. Finally, in 1899, she married a much younger man named Hugo Gerald de Bathe and retired to Monte Carlo. She lived there until her death in 1929.

The shade of the woman who appeared in the balcony of the Everyman Theatre could have belonged to Lily Langtry, although there was nothing in her past to suggest she would return from the other side. It could also have been that of Ellen Terry, who performed in this same theatre. This beloved theatrical legend first performed onstage playing 'Maxmillius' in Shakespeare's *The Winter's Tale* at the age of eight. Her parents were strolling players and she toured with them, learning her craft from her father who drilled her in clear elocution. She went on to perform many roles, including 'Puck' in *A Midsummer Night's Dream* and 'Ophelia' in *Hamlet*. She later formed a lasting alliance with Sir Henry Irving, playing 'Guinevere' in his production of *King Arthur*, among many other roles. Sir Bernard Shaw was enchanted by her and Oscar Wilde wrote a sonnet in her honour. She had a magnificent acting career, which lasted over fifty years. She died only a year after Lily Langtry and her ashes are interred in the actor's church, St Paul's in Covent Garden.

In Roger Manvell's biography of Ellen Terry he writes that when she died the streets of London were lined with people for sixty miles, many of whom left bouquets of flowers for Britain's queen of the stage. Her great acting legacy was handed down through her family, for her nephew became another stage and screen legend, Sir John Gielgud.

As with Lily Langtry there was nothing in Ellen Terry's life that would suggest a reason for her to return to haunt this lovely theatre. But could this shade belong to one or other of these two great ladies of the theatre, who perhaps like many actors could not resist the opportunity of hearing the tumultuous applause for their performances just one more time?

The theatre really came into its own during the Second World War as many theatres in London were closed. After the war, audience numbers dropped off sharply due to the reopening of the London theatres and the competition from movie theatres. When an announcement was made in 1959 that the New Theatre and Opera House would close, a public outcry led to the formation of the Cheltenham Theatre Association and to the raising of funds to save this well-loved cultural institution.

By May 1960 the building had been re-modelled and was given a new name – the Everyman Theatre. It became a repertory company and proved so popular that by the late 1970s an additional £3 million was raised to renovate the auditorium and the backstage areas.

In the mid-1990s the Everyman Theatre became a touring venue once again and to this day boasts an impressive variety of performances including drama, musicals, children's theatre and that evergreen of English theatrical highlights, the pantomime. The Everyman also produces many theatre programs that help members of the community explore their creative potential and hosts various civic outreach activities. The Everyman Theatre continues, after 117 years, to be one of Cheltenham's most popular cultural landmarks.

In addition to the shadowy spectre in the upper circle, eerie music has been heard coming from the stage of the Everyman. This music has been heard many times by a technician who worked at the theatre for over twenty years. These manifestations begin on the night of the full moon, and the sound starts high up near the roof in the backstage area, usually with just a few bars of music floating down to the stage level. Next, the source of the music will switch to another area and appear to be coming from the wings or beneath the stage. At first this music will move slowly from one location to another but then the tempo of the location changes and builds until everyone who witnesses this weird event will get a headache from the frenetic pace of these movements. In addition, it is very hard to identify the instruments that are creating the music as they are not like any from a conventional orchestra. The music has been described as an unearthly sound that makes such an impression on those who hear it that it is never forgotten.

When this phenomenon was first reported the idea that it might be a ghostly presence was dismissed. This strange sound was thought to be coming from the theatre's sound system or perhaps from a radio that was being played by an actor or a technician backstage. But after this music was heard on several occasions, all technical equipment was turned off and every square inch of the theatre was searched for a possible source. None was found and eventually it was acknowledged that the music must somehow come from another dimension.

Another area of the theatre that appears to be haunted is a section of the auditorium close to the main doors by the foyer. Witnesses of this haunting describe suddenly having an attack of 'pins and needles' followed by a terrible fatigue, almost as if all the energy has been drained out of their bodies. Next, faint music is heard. At first, of course, it is assumed that pre-show music is playing or perhaps a rehearsal song. But then there is a realisation that this music is actually coming from some other place as it is accompanied by a spine-chilling vibration. No one knows the origin of this unsettling event but it has happened many times and some of the more sensitive witnesses who have experienced it have actually had screaming terror fits and have fled the theatre shaking with fear.

5 The Suffolk Arms Poltergeist

The Suffolk Arms is a charming place to spend an evening. During the Cheltenham Festival it is crowded with punters, owners, tipsters and trainers who have just come over from the racecourse. The locals mix in too and everybody enjoys the jaunty live music and a menu of typical British pub food with Thai specialty dishes thrown in for variety. Altogether this hostelry, situated on Suffolk Street, has a very enjoyable ambience and is not far from Montpelier Square in Cheltenham.

Perhaps the poltergeist that inhabits the premises enjoys the fun liveliness of this pub too. No one knows the origins of this female ghoul, nor the reason why she is haunting the Suffolk Arms. Some people call her the 'Creepy Klepto' because many items have disappeared from the pub and she is thought to be responsible. Her playful kleptomaniac obsession leads to her stealing items and then replacing them just when the owner has given up on a search and decided that whatever is missing is gone for good.

On one occasion a new staff member who had not heard of the pub poltergeist descended to the cellar for supplies, unaware of what awaited him. The poltergeist must have been feeling particularly rambunctious that evening because the knocking and the laughter began and then increased in volume and tempo until it reached a frenzied cacophony of sound. This new staff member must have thought he had somehow wandered into a horror movie because after this experience he ran screaming from the building and never returned.

two

Prestbury

Introduction

Prestbury, considered one of the most haunted places in England, is a medium-sized village situated below the Cleeve Hill scarp. A boundary change in 1991 incorporated Prestbury into the borough of Cheltenham but it still retains all of its charming village characteristics, including picturesque thatched cottages and ancient public houses, most of which are built of honey coloured Cotswold limestone. The medieval Church of St Mary completes this bucolic picture together with numerous cottages that line the High Street, many of which are now used as shops. It also has fine examples of Georgian and Regency architecture.

The very first record of Prestbury dates from AD 899 and it is mentioned in the Domesday Book of 1086. At that time thirty-six people were recorded as living in the village. Prestbury was first known as Preosdabyrig which translates as 'the priest's fortified dwelling'. By the mid-thirteenth century it was known as a prosperous market town on the route between Winchcombe and Gloucester.

In those long-ago days markets were generally at least a day's journey apart and as Cheltenham had been operating a market for some time, after being granted permission to do so by Henry III in 1226, it was considered unusual when the Bishop of Hereford gained permission for nearby Prestbury to have its own market and fair in 1249. This market was situated by The Burgage, a curious name for one of the streets that leads up to Cleeve Hill. Burgage was an ancient form of tenure established in the thirteenth century and refers to how property and land were legally held in those times. Tenants were allowed to live upon their plot of land, which usually included a house, in return for economic services, military service or money. Rural land was more often than not allowed to be held in return for services rather than for money.

As English property lines have often remained unchanged over a long period of time, the extensive frontages and long, narrow plots that typify these burgages can still be seen in Burford, Oxford and Chipping Camden in addition to those in Prestbury.

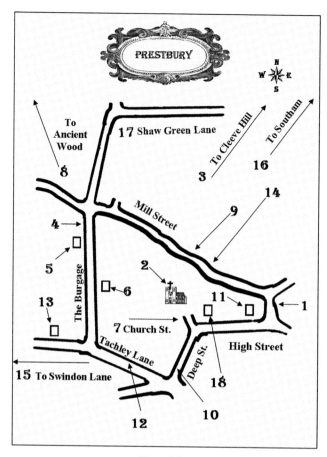

Key to Map

Story	Location	Story Title
1	Cleeve Corner	The Strangled Shade of Cleeve Corner
2	St Mary's Church	Ley Lines and the Black Abbot
3	Cleeve Hill	The Cleeve Hill Haunting
4	The Burgage	The Decapitated King's Messenger
5	Sundial Cottage	The Sad Shade of Sundial Cottage
6	Prestbury House	The Poltergeists of Prestbury House
7	Church Street	The Photo Poltergeists of Prestbury
8	Ancient Wood	A Bargain with the Devil
9	Mill Street	The Grotto Ghouls
10	Deep Street	The Civil War Spectres
11	Morningside House	The Abbot of Morningside House
12	Tatchley Lane	The Peeping Thomasina of Prestbury
13	Walnut Cottage	Old Moses
14	Mill Street	The Plough Inn Poltergeists
15	Swindon Lane	The Shadowy Shade of Swindon Lane
16	Southam	The De La Bere Haunting
17	Shaw Green Lane	The Archer and the Soldier
18	High Street	The Kings Arms Hotel (See Introduction)

Another salient feature of Prestbury is the world-famous Cheltenham Racecourse, which was built here in the early 1800s. The well-known Cheltenham Gold Cup meeting is held at the Cheltenham Racecourse with members of the royal family often in attendance.

In the 1750s Prestbury had its own venue to 'take the waters' named Hyde Spa, which today is Hyde Farm in the west part of the village. Over a period of 100 years beginning in the eighteenth century, Prestbury was a thriving spa resort for Cheltenham visitors looking to improve their health. Also the Grotto Tea Rooms in Mill Street was considered, at that time, to be a very desirable place to take tea and host dinner parties.

Until the 1930s, trams ran the length of Prestbury High Street on their way to the top of Cleeve Hill. The sharp bend at the end of the High Street created a need for workers to constantly grease the rails, thus preventing the outside wheel of the tram from vibrating as it took the corner.

A casual stroll around this charming village on a sunny day gives no hint of the horrors that took place within its borders. However, ghost hunters should beware of the locales described below.

1 The Strangled Shade of Cleeve Corner

Ahhhhhhhh! A terrifying, bone-rattling scream pierced the air. This scream was immediately followed by a muffled thump. But the next sound was different. A neighbour who heard the scream had been washing up her breakfast dishes at the time – it was barely dawn but her husband always made an early start. She stopped what she was doing, stood completely still and listened intently. After a few moments she could identify it. Yes, it was a woman, she thought, who was still trying to scream but was being stifled by an assailant. Soon the muffled screaming gave way to horrific choking sounds. The neighbour tried to shake the notion that someone was being strangled. Things like that just didn't happen. Not in Prestbury, anyway. Eventually the choking sounds stopped, leaving only silence. After a while the dish-washing witness convinced herself that she was reading too much into what might have been a few kids playing around or perhaps even a cat fight in one of the alleys.

But sometimes things like that do happen, even in the sleepy little village of Prestbury.

When they found her, still and lifeless on the bed, they shook their heads. She was beautiful and almost looked as if she was still sleeping, except for the man's necktie that was knotted tightly around her neck. Yes, she had been strangled alright. Her elegant bridal gown of ivory satin was laid over a chair, for she had been married only the day before. Gifts were piled up in various places around the house. Many of their bright shiny wrappings remained undisturbed for most of them had not yet been opened.

St Mary's Church, Prestbury.

Poltergeist-ridden Prestbury High Street.

The bride's headdress had been laid on a dresser the night before. She must have clutched at it in desperation as she tried to push away her attacker. It lay crumpled and forlorn on the floor, its small, white lace flowers now crushed and sad. Much of her bedroom was in disarray, looking as if it had been ransacked.

This all happened in Victorian times in a rambling old house near Cleeve Corner, which is not far from St Mary's Church, but no one was ever arrested for this terrible crime. Some said that this woman was murdered for her jewellery and her wedding gifts. But many of the gifts were undisturbed. Others say that she was strangled by her new husband after he received her dowry.

The bride who suffered this horrible death returns as a spectre and repeatedly relives this terrible ordeal. Many inhabitants of Prestbury who pass Cleeve Corner experience a horrific feeling of being strangled and are forced to share this ghastly experience with the long-dead bride.

Also, those who stay in the same room as the bride have been haunted on many occasions. When a visitor retires all may seem well, but in the middle of the night the guest will be awoken with a terrible feeling of unease and impending disaster. Some have described this feeling as 'pure evil'. After this atmosphere has taken hold an otherworldly light illuminates the entire room and the temperature drops alarmingly. Those who have braved a night in this room cannot describe these next events without breaking down. After the strange light fades, a deep vibration sets up what seems to be an electrical charge. Flashes of static electricity zing around the room and make sizzling noises as they strike metal objects. Next, invisible hands reach out from some other dimension and begin squeezing the visitor's neck. Instinctively, the victim reaches up to pull these violent hands away but finds nothing there. However, the squeezing continues. At first it is a gentle grasp but then the pressure increases until the victim blacks out. When this poor soul awakens some time later everything appears normal; that is, until he or she looks in the mirror. The horrible sight that greets the victim of this haunting is a ring of bruises around the neck.

So ghost hunters take a big gulp of air and hurry past Cleeve Corner, or you may find the next breath you take will be your last!

2 Ley Lines and the Black Abbot

It is not surprising that the village of Prestbury is considered one of the most haunted places in England as it is located on an intersection of the mysterious network of prehistoric pathways that cross the country, known as ley lines. These ley lines, or dragon lines as they are sometimes called, are strange phenomena that are thought to alter the earth's magnetic field.

In 1921 Alfred Watkins, an avid photographer, was seized by a sudden realisation as he gazed at a map of the Herefordshire countryside. He noticed that all the important ancient spiritual sites were connected by absolutely straight lines. Watkins researched these straight lines crossing the countryside and subsequently wrote books and gave talks on his findings. He expounded his theories in his book *The Old Straight Track*, published in 1925. Adherents of his theory formed the 'Straight Track Club' in 1930 and set about finding and recording a network of these straight lines all over Britain. Watkins called these straight tracks 'ley lines', which in Anglo-Saxon means 'strips of land that have been cleared'. Watkins maintained that these tracks had been formed by traders of the Neolithic period and observed that they travelled along ridges from one hill summit to another. In addition, they sliced through every kind of country including thick forest and deep valleys. Watkins was not the first to expound the theory of ley lines, however, as similar ideas had been put forward from the eighteenth century onwards by French, German, British and American observers. These ley lines are often hidden under trees and vegetation and are frequently found by dowsing. This technique uses a divining rod to locate water or other objects or paths.

An article in *New Scientist* magazine published in 1987 suggested that many animals including pigeons, whales, bees and quite possibly bacteria use ley lines as a navigational tool. These various species find their way back to their breeding grounds or to warmer climates during winter months by using the lines as a compass. A tissue containing magnetite is apparently able to receive a signal from these ley lines that allows living creatures to register magnetic changes. This magnetite has been discovered in the tissue of humans in the ethmoid bone in the front of the skull. However, another theory instead suggests that ley lines are a complicated network of prehistoric trade routes.

According to *Harper's Encyclopedia of Mystical and Paranormal Experience*, ley lines are 'patterns of powerful, invisible earth energy that are said to connect various sacred sites, such as churches, temples, stone circles, megaliths, holy wells, burial sites, and other locations of spiritual or magical importance'.

It is well documented that technical equipment behaves in a strange fashion when used near ley lines, perhaps because of interference from electromagnetic fields. The sceptics dismiss the existence and importance of ley lines, but it seems too much of a coincidence that so many important historical, religious, spiritual, sacred and burial sites are located either on ley lines or at their intersections.

It has been proved that activity from electromagnetic fields can alter the body and the mind. Many people, especially perhaps the most sensitive, have on a number of occasions complained of a raft of symptoms in the vicinity of ley lines. These symptoms include a general feeling of unease, giddiness, severe migraines, nausea and mental illness. In recent times a woman from the Cheltenham area was stricken by an illness that no doctor could diagnose. Many of her symptoms were those typically associated with coming into contact with ley lines. She described a feeling of being haunted by something intangible but very powerful. Eventually it was discovered that the bedroom of her house was located at the intersection of several ley lines. When she moved her bed to another room in the house her symptoms disappeared.

It seems that some ley lines are considered beneficial and others appear to be detrimental. Prehistoric shamans had a great understanding of the location of those beneficial lines and chose the sites of sacred buildings in order to provide a harmonious environment for the construction of spiritual structures.

There are a number of maps of these ley lines, some of which conflict with each other. It is generally held that in Britain, however, that one of the four Long Stones in the Forest of Dean is a central connecting point for them all. Ley lines could also be connected to long-used footpaths that have been established by the constant tread of pilgrims and wayfarers through the ages. These mysterious routes could also have a spiritual connection with the suffering of those who found a need to use these secret passages for their escape from their enemies, or perhaps from religious persecution.

According to Danny Sullivan's book *Ley Lines*, this could have been the case with the Black Abbot of Prestbury who can be seen haunting Prestbury at Easter, Christmas and on All Saints Day. Sullivan states that the Black Abbot starts his walks at the church in Prestbury, goes through the churchyard and ends at Reform Cottage in Deep Street, a partly weather-boarded house dating from the sixteenth century, which was most likely a converted barn. Paranormal activity is supposed to occur in the village when the old monk is about.

The garden of Reform Cottage is said to lie over the burial grounds of the monks who came to Prestbury Priory from Llanthony Secunda Priory in Gloucester, and a secret passageway is supposed to link the cottage with the church. One of the cottages nearby was once the vicarage and after many hauntings was exorcised by the Church. Meanwhile, it is perhaps no coincidence that Llanthony Priory is situated on a ley line that connects with St Mary's Church in Prestbury.

It is also no coincidence that Llanthony Priory is said to be haunted by several of the monks who inhabited it until the Dissolution of the Monasteries in 1538, during the reign of Henry VIII. This Augustinian priory is located in the remote and isolated Vale of Ewyas in the Black Mountains region of the Brecon Beacons National Park in Monmouthshire, south-east Wales. It is seven miles north of Abergavenny on the road to Hay-on-Wye and is mostly in ruins. It has now been graded as an Ancient Monument.

Building work was begun around the year 1100 by Norman nobleman William de Lacey, who restored a ruined chapel on this site, later expanding it to a full church. His devotion attracted a band of followers and together with them he consecrated the church in 1108, dedicating it to St John the Baptist. Later, in 1118, a band of forty monks who had come from England founded an Augustinian priory on the same spot.

Reform Cottage, Prestbury, home of the Black Abbot's shade.

The shade of the Black Abbot has been seen here.

The connection with Prestbury was made after these monks were repeatedly attacked by the local inhabitants, thereby forcing the monks to return to Gloucester where they created another cell called Llanthony Secunda. The aforementioned Black Abbot who haunts Prestbury Church is said to have been a member of this cell.

Today the ruined Llanthony Priory, surrounded on three sides by mountains and miles from any town, is occupied by a hotel situated in the one tower that remains intact. When the wind whistles through the mountain passes and the mists swirl around the high peaks, this hotel becomes a very creepy place, with the owner reportedly hearing many a loud bump in the night. Perhaps the priory is haunted by the Black Abbot, who divides his ghoul-like visitations between Llanthony Priory and Prestbury.

In addition to his visits to Reform Cottage, the Black Abbot's apparition has been seen to walk the aisles of St Mary's Church in Prestbury. He has made numerous appearances, one of which startled the vicar who one day found the Black Abbot's spectre sitting on a gravestone. The abbot has scared so many of the parishioners that the church itself has had to be exorcised.

The Black Abbot haunted a local vicar here in Prestbury.

It is thought that this exorcism, conducted by the vicar of St Mary's, chased away the ghost of the Black Abbot by using the ritual of 'bell, book and candle'. As this medieval method of exorcism begins, the church bells are rung, a religious book, usually a Bible, is ceremoniously slammed shut after which a lighted candle is snuffed out. Everybody who has gathered to take part in this ceremony is asked to chant the words 'ring the bell, close the book, quash the candle'.

St Mary's Church is well suited to its role as the central feature of the most haunted village in England. It dates back to the twelfth century and has seen more than its share of changing religious fortunes. The church's architectural features include a chancel, nave, north and south aisles, west tower, south porch, and north and south vestries.

The church has been altered many times, but it is known that in 1698 it had a north entrance and porch. The roof-line of the porch can still be seen. Also in this year buttresses were added to the tower. The tower was begun in the thirteenth century and was completed, or perhaps partially rebuilt, in the late fourteenth century, resulting in four stages with an embattled parapet and gargoyles at the angles.

These gargoyles seem to attract ghosts as they often consist of carved faces showing horrific expressions. Other examples include screaming monsters, serpents, devils, centaurs, daemons, cretins and fire-breathing dragons. The word gargoyle is thought to be a translation of the French word *gargouille*, which means 'to gargle'. Often decorating the exterior and interior of churches, gargoyles were originally used as

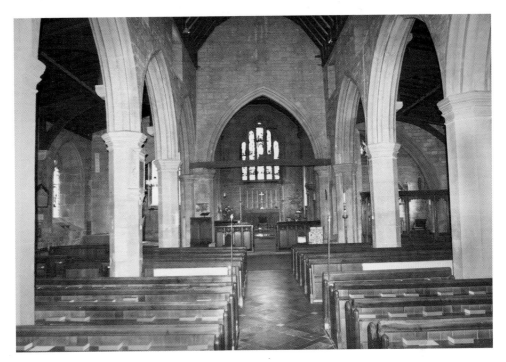

Interior of the exorcised St Mary's Church, Prestbury.

rain spouts. Medieval stonemasons seemed to compete with each other in an effort to carve ever more grotesque visages. These gargoyles began to disappear after the innovation of downspouts in the eighteenth century.

Other grotesque carvings used as decoration on the inside of church walls and ceilings can be equally spooky. These include green men, usually sporting a maniacally menacing grin and surrounded by leafy vines; griffins with their razor-sharp claws, aquiline beaks and lion's bodies; misericords, strange beastly figures depicting monsters carved on the hinged seats at the end of church pews; hunky punks, grotesque depictions of animals on their haunches; and chimeras, usually monsters comprised of monks, limbs of animals and flame-snorting humans. On more than one occasion parishioners of these medieval churches have glanced up during a long sermon and glimpsed what appears to be a spectre as it lurks in the dark gloom of the church ceiling, hiding among the carved faces of the gargoyles.

St Mary's Church was built in both the Early English and Perpendicular styles of architecture and was restored by G.E. Street in 1864 at a cost of over £3,000. Fifteenth-century arcading, a chancel arch and a double piscina in the Lady Chapel grace this church, along with an embattled tower which sports eight bells, six of which were cast in 1748. The simple octagonal font was replaced at the time of this restoration by a more elaborate one of coloured marble with inlaid panels. New pews were also installed.

The Priory, the site of an ancient monastery.

A ghostly funeral cortege visited Cleeve Hill.

The windows of stained glass were mostly broken by the year 1700. A depiction in one of the lower windows on the south side of the chancel of John Wyche, Prior of Llanthony (1409-1436), is the only one that remains. A west gallery was added by the late 1790s to accommodate the growing congregation, and a north gallery was added by 1827. A large fissure in the south side of the tower meant that extra buttresses were needed to shore it up and these were built in 1824. In 1840 a new vestry was added to the north-east end of the church and a new west gallery was constructed in 1843.

The church displays some tablets dedicated to the De La Bere family whose manor was in Southam. The De La Bere family lends its name to the well-known hotel in Prestbury that has its own famous haunting and is described later in this book. A modern sister church, St Nicholas', is situated to the west of the parish. Llanthony Priory once owned St Mary's Church and a nearby fourteenth-century house called the Priory. The Priory became the rectory after the Dissolution of the Monasteries.

After St Mary's Church was exorcised the Black Abbot's apparition stayed away from the church itself and confined his strolling, spectral visits to the churchyard. He moves about with his head bowed, his dark cowl covering his face, and is described as gliding rather than walking, as if suspended above the ground. He follows the same path every year on visits at Easter, Christmas and on All Saints Day.

The abbot's ghost has also been seen on numerous occasions in many other parts of Prestbury. He especially favours the seventeenth-century Plough Inn in Mill Street, which is close by St Mary's Church, and his spirit has startled many a visitor as they raised a glass.

Occasionally after a funeral the Black Abbot prowls around the churchyard and sometimes, to the horrified gaze of a dozen or so witnesses, disappears through a wall in the High Street.

3 The Cleeve Hill Haunting

Haunted Cleeve Hill overlooks Cheltenham Racecourse, Prestbury and the village of Battledown. The spectacular views from its heights show beautiful vistas of the Cotswolds and, on a particularly clear day, the Severn Vale and the Malvern Hills. It is the highest point in the Cotswolds and also in the county of Gloucestershire, being 1,083ft above sea level. Cleeve Hill is the largest area of unenclosed 'high wold' in the Cotswold region. An Iron Age hill fort nestles on its western scarp and the Cotswold Way hiking trail leads across its limestone grassland and Middle Jurassic-period rocks.

On one occasion a teacher drove down from Cleeve Hill and clearly saw a Victorian funeral cortege making its stately way across a field next to the road. At first she did not realise that she was witnessing a spectral event, a very grand one in fact.

Victorian funerals were distinguished by their grandiose pomp and no holds were barred in giving a good send-off to a dearly departed loved one. A Victorian cortege

St Peter's Church on creepy Cleeve Hill.

made a magnificent sight. The hearse, an elegant high-wheeled, decorated carriage drawn by as many as six impressively tall carriage horses, sporting plumed, black ostrich feathers waving at their heads, would lead the procession while a line of carriages accompanied by attendants would follow.

The hearse in a top-of-the line funeral would have glass sides with silver and gold decorations and apparently this was just such a one on this day, as the witness distinctly saw the sun reflected off the silver and gold side panels of the hearse. Inside, the elm coffin would have lid ornaments and inscribed plates with a canopy of black ostrich feathers.

The hearse would be followed by a line of coaches carrying the mourners. With blinds drawn, all those inside would be sobbing into their black-edged handkerchiefs. The female mourners wore jet jewellery and dresses made of black silk grenadine or black gros grain with capes of crape-trimmed cashmere with jet trimmings. They also wore heavy black veils and gloves and carried large mourning fans made of black ostrich feathers with tortoiseshell handles. The men wore mourning suits with black crape armbands and top hats. If any of the mourners were associated with the military, full uniforms would be worn along with medals and decorations.

The cortege travelled slowly and foot attendants would accompany the mourners along with baton-carrying pallbearers. Because of the often bitter cold these foot attendants, sometimes called 'feathermen' as they carried black ostrich feathers during the procession, would be given gin to help them endure the long hours they would spend outside.

The result of this practice may have explained the comments made by the teacher who saw the spectral cortege. She said that she saw several men dressed in black who accompanied the hearse reeling around and laughing inappropriately. Apparently, it was often the case at Victorian funerals that a little too much gin was given to the attendants and as a result they became tipsy and misbehaved.

The teacher who witnessed the procession could not understand why the cortege was making its slow progress through a field and was not using the road. This observation gave even more credence to the fact that this was indeed a spooky recreation of a real Victorian funeral, because in those days it was often the practice for a funeral to take a different route from that used by the townspeople. This would keep evil spirits away from the paths that the living used every day.

The awe-inspiring sight of this cortege caused the witness to turn her car around on the Southam Road and return for another look. Although this was accomplished in a short amount of time, by then the cortege had completely disappeared. The teacher

St Peter's Church overlooks the site of the haunting.

was puzzled because there was no way that the procession could have reached the other side of the field so quickly. It was only when she actually got out of her car and walked around the field that it slowly dawned on her that she had witnessed a visitation from the other side. This realisation was accompanied by a severe drop in body temperature even though it was a sunny, warm day. This spooky event also gave the teacher nightmarish dreams of Victorian mourners, with skull faces, peering at her from the cortege for months to come.

4 The Decapitated King's Messenger

Perhaps the most famous of the many ghosts roaming around Prestbury is that of the king's messenger who lost his head during the English Civil War.

During this time Oliver Cromwell had arranged for many of his officers to be billeted in Prestbury House in The Burgage and had set up camp for himself close by. Meanwhile, just a few miles away, a band of Royalists were occupying an encampment on Cleeve Hill. Cromwell and his men knew that at some point a message would be sent to nearby Gloucester and he ordered that an ambush be set up.

Up on Cleeve Hill a king's messenger was sent to deliver an urgent note and galloped through Prestbury en route to his destination. His journey took him across The Burgage where he was spotted by Cromwell's forces. As they moved in for an attack the messenger urged his horse into a full gallop. Clods of earth were thrown up by the horse's hooves and the messenger would have easily outrun the pursuing Roundheads.

A Civil War soldier was decapitated here in Prestbury.

However, he was travelling so fast that he did not see the fine wire that was stretched between two stands of trees across his path. The unfortunate result was that this poor man's head was instantly severed from his body, making a gory sight indeed.

In the nineteenth century a skeleton was discovered during a construction project on this very spot and it was thought to belong to this hapless fellow.

From the day of this messenger's demise the disembodied sound of a galloping horse which has been heard on numerous occasions is attributed to the soul of this restless ghost. The fast rattle of a horse's hooves often disturbs the serenity of this peaceful spot, particularly at night. On other occasions a headless horseman is seen riding at full gallop wearing a Civil War uniform. These events never fail to fill any of those who witness them with a terrible shiver of fear followed by spine-chilling spasms of horror.

5 The Sad Shade of Sundial Cottage

At first the pretty young girl with light brown hair and clear blue eyes cried heartrending sobs that filled all those who heard them with great sadness She was seated on an elegant seventeenth-century chair and her little white lace handkerchief appeared to be quite wet through as she mopped at the ever-flowing tears. Later she sat silent and still in her long gown, but the tears still ran down her cheeks and seemed to mingle with the rain that fell softly outside. Next, she stood up and wandered around the room, walked over to the window and pulled the curtains aside. For what seemed like an eternity she stared mournfully out into the street as if looking for someone. Her eyes searched as her head moved from side to side but nobody came for her. Eventually, she moved over to a musical instrument that looked something like a piano. This had magically appeared in a corner of the room and she sat down on a stool in front of it. She leafed through sheet music that was propped up above the keys and, after selecting a tune, began to play. She played beautifully and the old fashioned instrument made a sweet sound, as if in accompaniment to the falling rain. This girl appeared to be singing but no sound was heard. When she had finished she walked back to the window and resumed her searching and her sobbing. An aura of terrible sadness pervaded the entire room. Presently, almost imperceptibly, the lovely young girl who had by now sobbed her heart out gradually faded away until she completely disappeared.

This scene was witnessed by a London family who had fled the Blitz during the Second World War and had taken up residence in Sundial Cottage. The horrors of the bombing suddenly seemed to pale in comparison to this haunting taking place in the living room of this ancient building.

The London family had been rendered wide-eyed with terror when this young girl's spectre had appeared and they had remained frozen in spine-tingling silence as this long scene unfolded before them. This poor family's nerves were already shredded

Haunted Sundial Cottage in Prestbury.

by their experiences in London and when they took Sundial Cottage they had no idea that it was haunted.

When they had recovered somewhat from this ghoulish manifestation, notes were compared and it was found that all the members of the family had a strong feeling that this sad and beautiful shade, who appeared to be no more than eighteen years of age, was lovelorn. They all 'knew' that she was bereft over the loss of a young lover even though no words had been uttered by her during the haunting.

Sundial Cottage is a quaint and charming seventeenth-century, whitewashed, three-storey house located on The Burgage in Prestbury and has a Welsh slate roof and dormer windows.

The strange, old-fashioned musical instrument that the young girl played during the haunting turned out to be a spinet. These harpsichord-like instruments are thought to have been invented by Hieronymus de Zentis in 1631 and were known in France as the *epinette a l'italienne*. The word spinet comes from the Italian *spinetta*, which was used in seventeenth-century Italian to describe quilled musical instruments. Spinets had smaller soundboards than harpsichords and a softer tone. The spinet was not meant for concert use but was ideal for the home as it was relatively inexpensive and did not take up a great deal of space. In the seventeenth and eighteenth century, young ladies of refinement all learned to sing and play musical instruments. The young lady whose spectre had visited Sundial Cottage must therefore have come from a fairly prosperous family as she was very accomplished musician.

Nobody seems to know the full story of this young girl's demise or why she has joined the ranks of the undead. It is thought that her feelings for her lost love are so strong that her soul cannot rest until she finds him and, therefore, she returns again and again in a fruitless search.

The London family was one of many who had been scared out of their wits by this young lady's visits, for this same spectre had made numerous appearances during the nineteenth century.

A sad shade once played her spinet here.

Imagine sitting quietly in the living room of the cottage, perhaps with a cup of tea in hand, reading the morning newspaper when not a yard away a young girl suddenly appears crying tears of unimaginable regret. This sad, sobbing shade has been the cause of many a chilled spine, momentarily stopped heart and spilled cup of tea in spooky Sundial Cottage.

6 The Poltergeists of Prestbury House

Today Prestbury House is a very comfortable, Grade II-listed, privately owned Cotswold Country Manor House Hotel. It is so comfortable, in fact, that a number of ghosts have taken up residence there and seem to enjoy staying in the hotel just as much as the guests do. It is perhaps no surprise that these ghosts have a hard time leaving as this hotel has wood-panelled rooms, roaring log fires in winter, croquet on the lawns in summer and, as a backdrop, the halcyon Cotswolds Hills.

Stephen Whitbourn, the current owner of the hotel, kindly showed the author around his beautifully run establishment and the lovely surrounding grounds that are haunted by several entities. Mr Whitbourn was most helpful and knew about many of the ghosts mentioned in this story and, in addition, was able to point to where the haunted Grotto Tea Rooms once stood (see the story 'The Grotto Ghouls', also in this chapter). This location can be seen from the grounds at the back of Prestbury House.

Prestbury House, where things go bump in the night.

The ghost of a child is heard and sometimes seen in and around Prestbury House. She laughs, frolics and even turns cartwheels as if enjoying herself very much. She appears to be about seven years old. She has been seen wearing clothes that place her in the seventeenth century.

Another frequently experienced spooky phenomenon is guests at the hotel hearing the sound of horses' hooves galloping through the grounds. Sometimes these sounds evoke real horses so effectively that guests become fearful of being trampled. These horses from the other side visit at night too and cause a particularly chilling sound on a cold winter's eve when there is a full moon. Some say that these horses belonged to a member of the Gorrie and Whitbourn familes. These two families, one English and the other Scots, once owned Prestbury House. At one time in the long-distant past, these two families fought – apparently to the death – but now several centuries later their descendants are united in peaceful wedlock.

Prestbury House is of a William & Mary design and sports a fine Georgian addition. This added wing was built approximately 250 years ago and nowadays houses the Georgian and Oak Rooms which are currently used as a breakfast room, bar, lounge, library and polo room. The original coach house is about 50ft from the main house and has been converted into accommodations. Prestbury House is one and a half miles from Cheltenham town centre and commands panoramic views of Cleeve Hill from its main reception rooms and grounds. Cheltenham Racecourse's main grandstand is a twenty-minute walk from the main entrance and the back straight of the course is at the bottom of The Burgage. The house stands in an acre of garden and five acres of grounds.

These grounds and gardens are also haunted by a very pretty servant girl who appears to come from a far distant time, perhaps from an era long before Prestbury House was built. Some say she is from the era of the Roman occupation or even earlier. Her strange garments make it hard to place her in time. She is always seen wearing the same dress; a rough, long gown made from a hemp-like material and swathed in a peculiar manner. She is always barefoot and wanders about forlornly with an ancient clay water pitcher in her hands. She never pours the water but instead stares into the distance as if eternally looking for someone or something. Sometimes witnesses have heard her gasp as if she were about to burst into tears but she has never been heard to say anything or cry out. Many of the visitors who have stayed at Prestbury House have seen her and tell of the air temperature dropping remarkably about half an hour before she makes an appearance. The body temperature of those who have experienced her manifestations drops as well, and some are left chilled for many hours afterwards.

Another ghoul haunting Prestbury House is the aforementioned Black Abbot of St Mary's Church, who wanders along The Burgage through Mill Street and back to St Mary's, which adjoins the grounds of Prestbury House. He has been seen by many hotel visitors and his sudden appearances and disappearances are sometimes attributed to the rumour that a tunnel exists leading from Prestbury House to St Mary's Church,

Many ghouls haunt Prestbury House, now a hotel.

although no tunnel has ever been found. There is some dispute as to whether this hooded monk is actually the ghost of the Black Abbot or the shade of some other poor monk who is also one of the wandering undead.

The third manifestation in the grounds frequently takes place in a spinney located a short distance from the west wing of Prestbury House. This strange haunting seems to recreate a ghostly tea party that was once held there when King George III hosted a gathering of family and friends. Tea was a novelty at this time, as it had only recently been introduced to England. The East India Co. first imported tea to England in 1689 and for the next 100 years it was extremely expensive.

King George's tea party in the spinney is made more believable by the fact that at this time tea was regarded as a luxury beverage that was fit only for Chinese emperors and kings.

George III reigned from 1760-1820 and in 1762 built Buckingham House in London, which has since been rebuilt and is now known as Buckingham Palace. King George met his wife, Duchess Sophia Charlotte Mecklenburg-Strelitz, on their wedding day, but despite the fact that they were total strangers at the time of their marriage it is known that these two royals enjoyed an extremely happy marriage. The king never took a mistress, which was the usual habit of the monarchs of those days, and he and Queen Charlotte had fifteen children; nine sons and six daughters. Perhaps it is the apparitions of these children that were laughing and frolicking at the king's tea party in the spinney. The laughing voices of young children have been heard many times by hotel guests and a former owner's dogs displayed a sudden change in behaviour in the vicinity of this spinney.

King George suffered several debilitating illnesses, both physical and mental, and in the latter part of his life his doctors were at a loss to know the exact nature of his maladies. His recurrent bouts of mental illness caused him and his family great distress and subsequently physicians who have studied his symptoms have suggested that he could have suffered from the blood disease porphyria. Finally, he was so disabled that he was unable to continue his rule and in 1810 a regency was established. George's eldest son, then Prince of Wales, was substituted as Prince Regent.

It is also known that King George made frequent trips to both Prestbury and Cheltenham spas to 'take the waters', an action, no doubt, carried out in order to cure his mysterious illnesses. Perhaps the haunting in the spinney by a spectral King George, Queen Charlotte, their children and guests manifests itself so that this royal family may relive those happier times.

In addition to this trio of hauntings, previous owners of the hotel talk of strange sounds that have been heard late at night. Distant calling voices, screeching sounds and deep rumblings have been heard coming from the ancient stone and timbers inherent in the structure of the building. Many attribute these disturbances to poltergeist manifestations as they are frequently accompanied by erratic temperature changes.

Prestbury House grounds, where royal shades take tea.

7 The Photo Poltergeists of Prestbury

Additional strange manifestations that frequently startle visitors to Prestbury are the shining orbs and scary ghost faces that appear in their holiday snapshots. These orbs and ghost figures are not seen through the viewfinder at the time that the pictures are taken, but when photographs are downloaded or developed these weird images show up in their dozens. At first mist seems to be covering the background of a holiday snap but upon closer inspection faces appear. These faces are fantastically ugly, almost like gargoyles or grotesques, or sometimes like skulls. It is possible to take a pen and outline the expressions of these spectral images to make them more distinct. If this is done, before very long the entire background of a photograph is covered in these horrifying faces.

The disembodied orbs that turn up in these photographs follow a similar pattern. When the orbs appear they are so prolific that many of them obliterate the background of a photograph. Their incandescent reflection overshadows everything in the foreground of a photo and at times they even appear to move around. Sometimes these orbs are white and at other times a ghastly green or ice blue.

Photographic experiments have been conducted to determine whether these photographs are fakes, but no camera tricks have been discovered. So many different visitors have encountered this problem that it would be impossible, if an attempt at faking the images were being made, to come up with the exact same representation in all of the various photographs.

Visitors will take pictures elsewhere with exactly the same camera equipment and not find anything wrong with their photographs. Some visitors who are superstitious have thrown away their photography equipment and started anew.

Nobody knows why these images appear or what they mean, but they turn up with spine-chilling regularity. Perhaps the ghosts of Prestbury are just having a little fun as they cross over to this side or perhaps these images that invade visitors' photographs are some kind of warning – one that is perhaps too terrifying to interpret.

8 A Bargain With the Devil

Cromwell visited Prestbury House, where some of his soldiers were billeted, on numerous occasions to give orders as his own staging post was just a few yards down the road. This revolutionary is said to have had his own ghostly visitation which caused him, some say, to sell his soul to the Devil.

J.A. Brooks refers to this legend in his book *Ghosts and Witches of the Cotswolds* and the following story is also well documented in other publications.

Cromwell, the son of a country gentleman, was born on 25 April 1599 in Huntingdon and became such an accomplished military leader that by the time he had routed the Cavalier forces at Marston Moor in 1644, he had earned the soubriquet 'Ironside'.

Cromwell was about to fight the Battle of Worcester and he felt it was imperative that he win, for this would give him the upper hand against King Charles II's forces and help bring an end to the Civil War.

On the morning of 3 September 1651, the very day the battle was about to begin, Cromwell summoned the captain of his regiment, Colonel Lindsey, and ordered him to join him on a short journey. Together the two men galloped to a wood a mile or two distant from their army's headquarters.

Colonel Lindsey later recounted that he had no idea of the purpose of this trek to the dark and eerie wood, but as soon as he entered he was overcome with the most terrible feeling of foreboding. After reaching the centre of the wood Cromwell held up his hand and both men came to a halt.

Presently, an old man appeared. At least, Colonel Lindsey thought he was seeing an old man until this figure drew closer. Lindsey peered through the impenetrable gloom of the wood and realised that, under his hat, this bent figure possessed no face at all, merely the image of a skull. The old man was a ghost and Lindsey was terrified. He instinctively pulled his horse's head around, making ready to flee, but Cromwell grabbed the bridle and stopped him. Cromwell berated Lindsey for his cowardice. This humiliated Lindsey, for he was a brave soldier in battle, but the evil atmosphere that emanated from the wood that day caused even his nerve to break. He waited in great fear as Cromwell then bargained with the ghost of the old man, who turned out to be the Devil himself.

The Devil agreed to guarantee a victory in the upcoming Battle of Worcester if, in return, Cromwell would give up his soul in seven years. Cromwell was furious and argued vehemently for twenty-one more years of life before the Devil took him. But the Devil would not move on his offer. Eventually Cromwell agreed and a deal was struck. Immediately, the ghost of the old man disappeared in a wisp of smoke and Cromwell, now drunk with power in anticipation of his future victory, let out an impassioned battle cry and galloped back to his army's encampment.

Lindsey, meanwhile, was still shaking with fear and after his first foray in the battle found himself unable to continue. He deserted the fight and made his way to Norfolk. There he sought the counsel of a parson, a Mr Thorowgood, who recorded everything that Lindsey recounted. Lindsey told of all that had transpired between Cromwell and the Devil and this was duly written down by the parson. Much later the consequences of this terrible bargain were noted by him too.

Cromwell was victorious that day and the Battle of Worcester was won. He continued to fight until the final defeat of the Cavaliers at Naseby. Parliament eventually fell into disarray and Cromwell dissolved it and ruled England under the self-anointed title of Lord Protector of the Realm.

But on the seventh anniversary of the Battle of Worcester Cromwell suddenly felt a tap on his shoulder. He turned to see the face of the Devil, who had returned for

Cromwell's headquarters were here in Prestbury.

his prize. Cromwell died on 3 September 1658, exactly seven years to the day after this decisive battle.

Despite Cromwell naming his son Richard as his successor, the Commonwealth did not rule effectively and the monarchy was restored a mere two years later.

In the Guildhall at Worcester the decorations include a gargoyle that is thought to be Cromwell portrayed as the Devil. Many people who look at this gargoyle are said to have dreams of the day this terrible figure appeared in the wood – as the ghost of an old man who then reveals himself as the Devil.

9 The Grotto Ghouls

In 1784 an enclave was built in Prestbury's Mill Street which included a pavilion, grotto and Chinese temple, and these buildings were used as a tea-drinking house. By the nineteenth century the Grotto Tea Rooms had become one of the main attractions of the village. It evolved as a social centre for the local inhabitants and a convenient refreshment stop for visitors coming to take the waters at the local spa. This would most likely have been Hyde Spa nearby. The Grotto Tea Rooms was fancifully decorated with all manner of shells and fossils and its Gothic windows were fitted with brightly painted glass. The Friendly Society of Prestbury held weekly meetings at the tea house in those days and it was so successful that it was eventually turned into an inn. Some years later, however, the Grotto Tea Rooms was shut down and the building which housed it demolished by the authorities because, by this time, it had gone downhill and was known as a place of ill repute.

Perhaps some of the spectres who have been seen and heard in the Grotto Tea Rooms' vicinity were once customers who enjoyed its ambience. There have been reports of raucous laughter and sounds of party-making coming from this same location on Mill Street. Some of the witnesses of these hauntings have talked about their encounters with the ghosts in question, and when all their descriptions were compared eerily similar images recurred. These witnesses talked repeatedly of the ghosts' strange, old-fashioned clothing of a sort no longer worn today.

The witnesses made sketches of the clothing worn by these ghosts but it was difficult to pinpoint their era from these drawings, so a collection of illustrations of many different clothing styles throughout the centuries was assembled and shown to them. Ultimately, illustrations of clothing worn from 1790-1840 were the closest match to the garments worn by these ghosts. Regency is the name given to this style and it is similar to the costumes worn by Jane Austen's characters in dramatisations of her books such as *Pride and Prejudice* and *Sense and Sensibility*. The witnesses spent some time carefully studying the illustrations supplied and picked out the clothing and accessory items that most resembled what both the male and female ghosts had been wearing in this crowd of raucous apparitions.

According to one of the witnesses, a man called Steve who did not wish to give his last name, he managed a good look at one girl, a very pretty spectre, who wore what he described as 'a kind of nightdress looking thing'. This was most likely a typical frock of the period which would have been an Empire dress, whose style was inspired by the classical, diaphanous Greek and Roman dresses from antiquity. This pattern of dress had been adopted in Regency times, no doubt as a rebellion against the discomfort of the enormous circular skirts, hooped petticoats and lace-edged pantaloons of the previous era. As the pretty nightdress-wearing ghost laughed and joked with her companions she obligingly turned full circle so that Steve could see what she was wearing in detail. Her dress was of a very simple design and consisted of a high-waisted frock that followed the wearer's figure and was made of muslin (soft cotton). Steve said that a 'bustier thing' was part of the design of the dress. This would have been a corded corset that fitted above the high Empire waist that supported her bust and was most likely decorated with a variety of frills, ruches, ruffs, shawls and feathers to make the low cut of the dress a little more modest where necessary. Steve also described the dress as having 'kind of lacing like Queen Elizabeth in olden times'. He would have been referring to spiral lacing used to tighten the bodice. He said this ghost was wearing 'a funny hat – a bit like from *Mutiny on the Bounty* only made of straw'. This may have been a typical style for women's hats of that time, namely a

Where the haunted Grotto Tea Rooms once stood.

bicorne hat, and underneath it her hair would have been pinned up and dressed at the back with a circle of curled ringlets. These had probably been fashioned with a curling iron. Steve particularly noticed her jewellery, which he described as 'a purple looking cross on a chain'. This would have been gold chain with a cross made of amethyst. This semi-precious stone was very popular during Regency times.

Steve felt that this particular ghost almost knew that she was being watched by someone from the other side and was very proud of her appearance. He said that she wore no make-up. This signified that she was from a prosperous family as apparently, in this era, it was considered inelegant to wear rouge which was all that was available at that time. This ghost almost seemed to be flirting with Steve and he said that she made the most of her accessories, pulling up her elbow-length gloves to show them off, fluttering her fan coquettishly and opening, closing and twirling her parasol many times. She was very petite and pranced around, giggling and laughing in her 'tiny ballet shoes' as Steve described her flat, soft, slippers until finally she opened 'a funny looking chain handbag'. This most likely would have been a metallic reticule, or evening bag, of the period. She then took out a small, lace handkerchief and waved it at him.

Steve was not the type to believe in ghosts and so he stepped forward to ask why the pretty apparition was dressed so strangely. As soon as he moved he noticed that a sudden drop in temperature chilled him and he felt paralysed. He was stopped dead in his tracks and at that same moment the ghost suddenly disappeared in a wisp of ectoplasm.

He found he could not move as the ectoplasm floated towards him and curled around his face. Finally, after about a minute, it dissipated and only then was he free to stride forward.

He was momentarily nonplussed but apparently his remarkable powers of observation were still intact because he then took note of what one of the other male ghosts was wearing. One male spectre strutted up and down Mill Street laughing uproariously, wearing what Steve described as 'a tail coat that men wear at weddings with the sides angled back and it had shiny lapels'. This ghost was most likely wearing a French cutaway style morning coat of corduroy and shot silk. These coats had broad revers, tight sleeves and a high collar, and were typically colour-coordinated in shades of brown and ivory. Steve said that the ghost was also wearing knee breeches, buckled shoes and knee-high stockings. Around his neck he was wearing a white, silk cravat and had on a wig, a tall top hat and carried a walking cane. Steve said that the spectre waved his cane around as he laughed and used it to rap on the ground. He also said the strangest thing was that although this spectre's laughter was loud, when his cane struck the ground it made no sound.

Steve still could not quite believe that this raucous crowd in front of him were ghosts and thought they must be on their way to a fancy dress occasion. He dismissed the pretty female ghost's sudden disappearance as some kind of magic trick. However, as the group of ghosts began walking down the street they walked right through him, finally convincing him that he had been a witness to a visitation from the other side.

This group of ghosts all dressed up in their elegant Regency finery seemed to have nowhere to go as they have been seen wandering along Mill Street many times. They appear to be looking for the Grotto Tea Rooms which, of course, was shut down some time before. But even when they cannot find their former meeting place their high spirits are not dampened. Many in Prestbury have heard and seen them laughing, joking, giggling and squealing.

Ghost hunters need not be afraid of these ghosts, who actually seem quite harmless. Perhaps the reason they seem so benign is because they appear to have just stepped out of the pages of a Jane Austen classic.

10 The Civil War Spectres

A terrace of three stone cottages in Deep Street, Prestbury, are each said to be haunted, but the one that concerns readers here is the middle of the three. This home has been visited on many occasions by several apparitions of Civil War soldiers.

These soldiers were reported to be Roundheads – the soubriquet given to the Puritan supporters of Parliament. According to John Rushworth's *Historical Collections*, the term was coined by an officer named David Hide who, during a riot, was said to have drawn his sword and proclaimed that he would 'cut the throat of those round-headed dogs that bawled against bishops'.

Undead Civil War soldiers visit cottages in Deep Street.

Apparently the Puritan Parliamentarians who opposed King Charles during the Civil War were called Roundheads, a pejorative term, because of their closely cropped hair. This was in contrast to the style of the Royalists with their much longer, more luxuriant locks. This difference illustrates the religious and social divide between the two factions that fought in the Civil War. However, another theory suggests that the Parliamentarians were called Roundheads because of the circular shape of their helmets. The Roundheads were for the most part devoted Puritans, ordinary men such as shoemakers, bakers, merchants, shepherds and the like, who wore simple clothes and fought with their Bibles tucked inside their uniforms.

The Civil War was prompted by an uprising of these Parliamentarians against the monarchy. It came to a head after King Charles attempted to dissolve Parliament when its members refused to follow his wishes. The Parliamentarians believed that Parliament should be run by the government, rather than the king, and were willing to die for their cause.

Their enemies, the Royalists, were given their nickname Cavaliers by the Puritans who used it to describe the reckless and arrogant nature of the followers of the king. However, a second theory claims that the Royalists were, in fact, called Cavaliers because they mostly fought on horseback and were identified by the French term for horse riders – *chevaliers*.

The Civil War began on 22 August 1642 in Nottingham when King Charles held up his standard as his men shouted 'God save King Charles and hang the Roundheads'.

Another ghost story in John Rushworth's aforementioned book, entitled *The Headless Horseman*, notes that Oliver Cromwell had some of his men billeted at Prestbury House, close to the stone cottage that is the subject of this next haunting. Perhaps this cottage had also been requisitioned for Cromwell's troops at the time. It is thought that the soldiers who inhabited it died a horrible death because their restless souls revisit this cottage on many occasions.

The hauntings began with rattling sounds of metal against metal. Nothing was seen by the inhabitants of the cottage at this time but further noises indicated that ghostly soldiers were suiting up for battle. At the time these men wore metal armour and steel helmets that protected their heads and faces.

Muttered voices were heard as the spectres of these soldiers handed each other various pieces of battledress and armaments. A typical Roundhead uniform would include a forged iron 'lobster tail' helmet with an articulated neck guard, ventilated ear covers and a frontal peak attached to a three-bar rigid faceguard. The earpieces would have leather loops allowing a tightened thong to secure the helmet under the chin.

The iron cuirass set, worn on the upper half of the body, included a heavy front chestplate with an iron backplate of slightly lighter construction. Leather shoulder straps held the cuirass in place and these were covered with iron plates. The front and rear plates would meet under the arms preventing any bullets from hitting their target. Soldiers who wore this outfit in Cromwell's New Model Army were also known as 'the Ironsides', and wearing this very effective armour helped them defeat King Charles.

The Roundheads were for the most part very religious and witnesses to this haunting say they also heard prayers chanted. In those long-ago times people spoke with a different dialect and the whispered prayers of these apparitions were difficult to understand.

Nothing more was heard in the cottage for the next three or four hours. After this time the home was suddenly filled with terrible cries of suffering and more prayers. It was then that shadowy figures of soldiers were seen for a fleeting second or two before suddenly disappearing. It would seem that these soldiers had returned after battle and some of them had been horribly wounded. Their pitiful cries continued far into the night and only slowly faded away with the dawn.

The poor people of Prestbury are forced to relive this fragment of the Civil War over and over as the restless souls of these soldier ghosts seem fated to continue their haunting through eternity.

11 The Abbot of Morningside House

This house in the centre of Prestbury, next to the car park, is thought to be haunted by an abbot in a black habit. There is much confusion about this abbot's apparition as many people assume that it is the same spectre as that of the Black Abbot of Prestbury who has long haunted St Mary's Church, the churchyard and many other locations in the town.

Perhaps this mystery can be solved by a description of the early history of Prestbury. In AD 899 the Bishop of Hereford established what was technically known as a palace in Prestbury along with many other palaces and manors throughout the country. The word 'palace' was used to describe the larger residences of bishops at that time, although some of these buildings were often not much larger than a typical manor house. In the late eleventh century an ecclesiastical enclosure consisted of a bishop's palace and other buildings used by the clergy. This palace would be separated from the priory and the churchyard and village dwellings would be clustered around this nucleus.

The remains of a moated hall, thought to be the Bishop of Hereford's palace or manor house, has been discovered on Spring Lane close to Cheltenham Racecourse. This site was excavated in 1966 revealing a fortified manor house in a complex of earthworks, including those of a great hall and kitchen. A large quantity of twelfth- and thirteenth-century pottery was also found at the site. In historical documents this site was known as Lower Noverton Moat, but it has since been built over.

The Bishop of Hereford who directed this palace to be built is thought to be Richard de Capella, bishop between 1121-1127, who also founded boroughs at his manors of Bromyard and Ledbury. He was keeper of the Royal Seal between 1107-1121 and knew the advantages to be gained from founding as many boroughs as possible.

Close to this date other boroughs were created, possibly by him, including Ross-on-Wye in Herefordshire and Bishops Castle in Shropshire. There was much competition at the time between other clergy and these boroughs may have been founded to win out over the Prior of Leominster as those created by him date from the same period.

The priory in Prestbury is close to the church and subsequently became a rectory after the Dissolution of the Monasteries by Henry VIII in 1539.

Bishops of this time toured their various palaces and manors, often with a large entourage consisting of over 100 men on horseback, and stayed for several weeks. These bishops also sometimes visited hunting lodges and would often have free privileges to hunt the area. Once the bishop arrived at one of his palaces or manor houses the hall became his feudal court. Here he would sit in baronial state to receive the homage of tenants, to dispense justice and threaten offenders with excommunication. Here he would also listen to the petitions of suitors to his court and preside over community festivities.

This historical evidence revealing the existence of a bishop's palace and priory indicates that there were many priests living in Prestbury over several centuries and therefore it is quite conceivable that the abbot who haunts Morningside Cottage is not, in fact, the Black Abbot of Prestbury.

There have been several accounts of hauntings by this particular abbot from the medieval era in addition to those of more recent times. These descriptions all recount one detail that distinguishes this abbot's characteristics from that of the Black Abbot.

Prestbury, the most haunted village in Great Britain.

All these witnesses talk of the terrifying and disgusting condition of this ghostly abbot's face and of how it changes into many different personas.

One witness, who does not wish to be named, described her encounter with the spectre known as the Abbot of Morningside House. This woman, who for the purposes of this story we shall call Jane, visited a friend who lived in the cottage. The custom at the time was for everybody to leave their doors unlocked. Jane arrived and, knowing she was expected by her friend, opened the front door and walked in. It was night-time and the passageway was almost completely dark, the only illumination coming from the room at the end of the hall where a small lamp shed a little light. Jane had only walked a few steps when a shadow moved in front of this lamp, blocking out the light almost completely.

Jane called out to her friend but received no reply. When she called a second time she heard only a deep, echoing growl in reply. She moved forward, peering into the gloom, and saw the silhouette of a monk-like figure with a cowl pulled down over his face. She was startled and screamed. With that this figure pulled the cowl away from its face and leered in a grotesque manner.

Jane froze in fear and watched as this hideously ugly monk's face transmogrified into a dozen different expressions, each taking on a more disgusting guise. One showed the spectre of a monk with his eyeballs hanging out of his head. Another showed his face covered with vicious cuts which oozed blood and yet another showed him with a huge, yawning, open mouth, which revealed foul, blackened and broken teeth. Jane almost fainted when another visage exhibited a horrible wound which had decimated most of the ghost's face. Blood was pouring from the wound and shattering screams of agony accompanied this sight. Next, this ghost's face changed to an image of a kindly old man but within seconds was covered in tiny, evil snakes with sharp fangs that first appeared as they slithered through the ghost's hair and crawled on to his face, taking bites out of him as they progressed.

Finally, Jane shook herself out of her paralysis and turned to run back along the passageway to the front door. When she turned the ghost of the monk was instantly before her, blocking her way through the front door. Jane sank to the floor in despair and as she did the ghost of the monk bore down on her with his last transmogrification, which showed his face slowly dissolving into a skull. The small snakes reappeared, now filling his empty skull, and began weaving in and out of his eye sockets. The terrifying screams of a thousand witch-like voices came from every corner of the passageway as the horrible skull moved closer and closer to Jane's face. At this point she collapsed into a dead faint. When her eyes opened, several minutes had passed and all was quiet. The ghost of the monk had disappeared but Jane was still trembling from head to foot. When she arose she ran screaming from Morningside House, never to return.

12 The Peeping Thomasina of Prestbury

Another famous spectre of Prestbury is a strange elderly woman who likes to look into windows. This peeping Thomasina has been seen many times, particularly on The Burgage and in Deep Street. She is a shadowy figure dressed in Victorian clothing, usually wearing a hoop-skirted dress of black bombazine with many petticoats, which is covered by a long, flowing, cloak of purple velvet edged in jet. She wears black-leather buttoned boots and long, leather gloves. Her taffeta bonnet is edged in lace and tied with a large bow under her chin. This makes her features difficult to discern but she is said to have a fine, handsome face. She carries a dainty parasol and often pulls out a lace handkerchief as soon as she spies somebody through a window. She dabs at her eyes and appears to be quietly sobbing all the way through her visitations. Perhaps she is looking for her lost family but she never seems to find them, although she has returned from the other side many times.

She has startled many residents of Prestbury when they glance out of the window to see her sad face peering inside. One witness dashed outside immediately after a haunting occurred and was quick enough to see this ghost fade into a wisp of ectoplasm. On other occasions she has been observed outside a house or a cottage as she creeps up to a lighted window at night. When she is challenged she disappears, sometimes reappearing a few minutes later.

This peeping Thomasina always seems to know where a gap in a carelessly pulled curtain will be. Some of the residents of Prestbury have taken to installing window blinds in addition to curtains to try and maintain their privacy. Many residents can sense her presence outside their windows even though their curtains are tightly drawn. This is because when this ghost is in the vicinity all present will feel a sudden drop in body temperature. Even on a hot summer day the spectre can chill an entire room and everybody in it within a few seconds.

One Prestbury resident found a lace handkerchief lying on the ground outside her window the morning after one of the ghost's chilling visits. This handkerchief was discovered to be from the Victorian era, although whether it actually belonged to this ghost or was put there as a prank has never been determined.

This ghost's appearances are particularly frequent around holiday times and her sobbing can actually be heard during these visits. Perhaps she misses her family so much that she cannot resist looking in on the cosy family scenes of holiday celebrations around a warm hearth. Some residents are touched by her predicament and try to invite her in to join them, but she simply fades away. It is the sincere hope of many in Prestbury that one day soon this sad shade will be reunited with her lost loved ones and her visits will no longer be necessary.

13 Old Moses

'Here's Old Moses, here I am'. These are the words uttered by a shade that has haunted Walnut Cottage in Prestbury on many occasions.

Walnut Cottage is a converted coach house and Old Moses particularly likes to visit the dining room. He seems to be a very benign spectre and his manner suggests that he is simply checking up on his earthly home and making sure that all is well. Perhaps he once lived or even worked on this spot when it was still a coach house. His pattern of speech and clothing suggest that this would have been in the seventeenth century, although it could have been even earlier. The various owners of Walnut Cottage now find his visits quite commonplace. These inhabitants were at first frightened by his sudden appearances but as they got to know this friendly shade a little better it was realised that he had no evil intention. His visitations are sporadic; sometimes coming in clusters of some frequency and at other times many years apart.

Although much research has been done to trace the origins of this ghost, nothing conclusive has been found. Witnesses have noticed that Old Moses seems to be fading in recent visits and suspect that he will not be around for much longer. Some inhabitants of the cottage have tried to engage him in conversation by asking him questions. He never directly answers but will try to pick up various items lying around the cottage as if he is fascinated by objects that were invented after his earthly lifetime.

The site of the Old Moses haunting, Prestbury.

His greeting is always the same and announces his arrival; towards the end of his visit he will only answer questions put to him with the following: 'You see, I likes to look in sometimes'.

14 The Plough Inn Poltergeists

There are many reports of the sound of ghostly horses' hooves heard galloping and cantering past the Plough Inn on Mill Street in Prestbury. No one knows the origin of this haunting, but it is thought that something terrible must have happened here at some point because this sound strikes fear into any animal that passes the inn. Local wags like to blame this spectral event on the strength of the beer consumed at this tavern and its effect on the witnesses' imagination. However, there is too much evidence to the contrary to give any credence to this theory. This haunting cannot be explained away that easily, for when herdsmen try to lead their sheep past the inn during these events this task can only be managed with the greatest difficulty.

All animals are extrememly aware of visitations by entities but sheep in particular are known to be very sensitive to any kind of otherworldly event occurring near them. When the horses' hooves are heard outside the inn these sheep become very agitated.

Cattle refuse to pass the eerie Plough Inn, Prestbury.

They set up a fearful squealing and back up in a desperate attempt to get away from the cause of their fright. These herds of sheep have even been known to injure each other during their attempts at flight.

Sometimes drastic measures are taken to drag these terrified animals back into the land of the living. On several occasions the herders tending the sheep have become 'infected' by the same strange manifestation and have also been rendered immobile.

Decoration on the exterior of the Plough Inn.

Inside the creepy Plough Inn, Prestbury.

The bar of the haunted Plough Inn.

Witnesses are said to have run away terrified after encountering the spooky image of a sheep herder and his sheep frozen in place.

On other occasions dogs and horses have been known, when passing the inn, to become wild-eyed and stop dead in their tracks, staying rooted to the spot as the sound of the cantering horses' hooves reaches them. Their paralysis goes very deep and it takes a lot of work by their owners to get them moving again.

15 The Shade of Swindon Lane

A spectral shepherd has been seen by a number of different witnesses driving his herd of sheep along Swindon Lane. This shepherd is dressed in what looks almost like rags and seems to have inhabited his earthly body a long time ago. His shadowy figure appears to be almost transparent, as do his sheep. Sometimes he disappears completely only to reappear again a few seconds later. Witnesses have been seen rubbing their eyes after catching a glimpse of him as his appearances can be so fleeting.

He keeps his head down and it is difficult to see his face under the brim of his battered hat. He has a stick or a crook with him and attends to his sheep just as a real-life shepherd would. He often seems to be in a tearing hurry, prodding his sheep along the lane as if he hasn't a minute to spare. He seems to call out to his sheep but no sound is heard coming from him.

Witnesses all have a similar story of the spooky sensation they experience when the spectral shepherd passes with his sheep. Silence descends on everyone and everything around those who are haunted by this vision. This is accompanied, on occasion, by an out-of-body experience.

One witness claims that during this haunting his spirit entirely left his body and zoomed up over the spectral shepherd and his sheep. This witness proceeded to have an out-of-body experience that gave him a bird's eye view of Swindon Lane and everybody in it, including himself! He felt as if he achieved some kind of weird cosmic consciousness and saw his earthly body standing just where his spirit had left it as it observed the haunting. He remembers clearly thinking that he needed a haircut because he could see his own body from behind. He also noted that he had a tear on the back of his jacket. When he drifted a little higher he could see in bedroom windows and over rooftops. He remembers being surprised by how many broken tiles were on a house in Swindon Lane.

Much research has been done on out-of-body experiences, a condition also known as astral projection, where apparently the spirit leaves the body. This syndrome usually occurs spontaneously, unless it is triggered by a seizure, surgery, a close-call accident, deep meditation, alcohol or drug use. Treatment with acupuncture can sometimes also bring on this condition. Out-of-body experiences are not a new phenomena but were

Spooky shades appear on Swindon Lane, Prestbury.

well documented by the Ancient Greeks and the early Egyptians who had a clear perception that life was multi-dimensional.

Dr Stuart Twemlow presented a dissertation on out-of-body phenomenology to the American Psychiatric Association in San Francisco, helping to prove that this condition was not a mental illness but a spiritually transformative experience. These research results showed that people who undergo out-of-body experiences were able to correctly identify surroundings at distant locations from their bodies and that this experience was not a dream or an hallucination. Apparently between 10-20 per cent of the population have experienced an out-of-body experience at one time or another.

Meanwhile, our poor witness continued to hover over the scene of the spectral shepherd for what seemed like an eternity. At first this fellow was scared, but after a while began to enjoy this strange sensation, describing it as akin to flying. He felt free of the normal constraints of earthly life, with no need to breathe or lift his heavy body. For a while he revelled in the euphoria produced by his complete freedom from gravity. Later, he experimented with steering his spirit, rather like a pilot steers a plane. He found that he could direct his perception anywhere he wanted to go and at first he whizzed up even higher until he could see the surrounding countryside for miles around. He could see right over Cheltenham and further to the rolling Cotswold hills. When he looked down he saw himself in the lane but now he was the size of a postage stamp. This was such fun that he decided to go to a still higher altitude. However, when he did he entered a cloud bank and then grew apprehensive as he could no longer see the ground. He descended again and as he did became aware of a new-found mental acuity. This gave him a feeling that his mind was then on a par with Einstein and that he had fallen through a hole in the time-space continuum.

This made him confident about his next decision, which was to fly down and be among the spectral shepherd and his sheep. When he arrived, however, he was gripped by a nameless fear that he likened to a vision of Hell. He realised that he had actually entered the same paranormal realm that the ghost was tuned into and was now subject to the horrifying events that had led to the haunting. He could not describe these events in specific detail; however, he did experience the horror of them. At one point he was aware that he was watching a succession of his past lives that he had never previously known existed. They buzzed through his consciousness at warp speed and sometimes in more detail than he cared to know. He said that he would never want to be subjected to that experience ever again.

After this he willed his consciousness to zoom back into his body but something was preventing him and he could not accomplish this. At this point he panicked and had an image of remaining among the undead forever. Then he noticed his real life body slowly walking away from the spectral shepherd and his sheep. He followed 'himself' as he strolled down Swindon Lane. After his body had travelled about 25yds he tried once again to enter it and this time he was successful. Later, he realised that his body had had the good sense to move out of the charged atmosphere of the haunting and it was this phenomenon that had earlier prevented him from re-entering his body. This witness stated that those few minutes on Swindon Lane were both the most exhilarating and the scariest he had ever spent in his entire life.

16 De La Bere Hotel Haunting

This fifteenth-century Tudor Manor House Hotel was once a girl's school but today is a very elegant hostelry with bedrooms named after kings and queens of England. Other historic names are used in the courtyard rooms which recall this building's long heritage.

Situated in Southam, it is approached via a tree-lined driveway and set in beautiful gardens with sweeping lawns, tennis courts and spectacular views over Cheltenham's famous racecourse. This romantic hotel, with its traditional Welsh slate roof, stone-mullioned windows and a tower or two, has kept much of its period atmosphere intact. It was once the home of Lord Ellenborough, a former Governor-General of

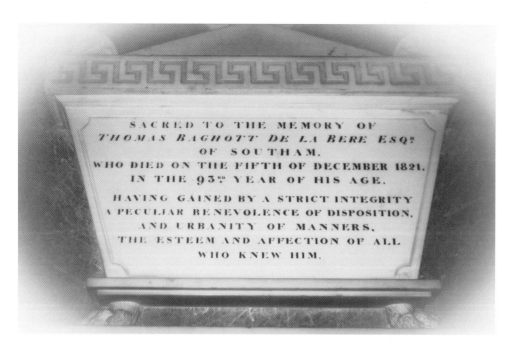

SACRED TO THE MEMORY OF
THOMAS BAGHOTT DE LA BERE ESQ!
OF SOUTHAM.
WHO DIED ON THE FIFTH OF DECEMBER 1821.
IN THE 93RD YEAR OF HIS AGE.

HAVING GAINED BY A STRICT INTEGRITY
A PECULIAR BENEVOLENCE OF DISPOSITION,
AND URBANITY OF MANNERS,
THE ESTEEM AND AFFECTION OF ALL
WHO KNEW HIM.

The De La Beres once owned a haunted manor.

India, and is an excellent spot for any visitor wishing to stay in a charming Cotswold village at the foot of majestic Cleeve Hill. It was inherited by the De La Bere family, who gave their name to this lovely manor, which was built in 1485. The De La Bere family crest still enhances many of the hotel's stained glass windows, particularly those in the Beaufort Restaurant on the ground floor.

Back when this hotel was a girls' school a tragic suicide resulted in frequent hauntings that sometimes gives the hotel guests of the present day spine-chilling scares.

A school matron known for her strict ways was in charge of the girls at the school and zealously ruled over her students both day and night. Even when the girls were sleeping this matron would frequently make inspections to be sure that none of them were perhaps secretly indulging in an innocent midnight feast or other such girlish misdemeanours. Apparently, this matron must have been suffering from some kind of mental illness for her inspections became more and more frequent and she began accusing the girls unjustly of various violations of the school's rules. The girls were at first too frightened to complain and as time wore on this matron became more and more tyrannical. Eventually, however, word leaked out to a few of the girl's parents that all was not well at the school. An investigation was called for and the matron was found out. She protested her innocence but it was of no use because, after complaints were made, the school authorities had been spying on her and already had evidence of her misdeeds. She was sacked from her job and was so mortified and despondent that she hanged herself in her bedroom.

This bedroom is located over what is now the hotel bar. This and a number of other rooms are haunted by the ghost of the matron to this day. Some hotel guests have encountered the spectral matron parading down the corridors on her way to checking on her girls to make sure they are sleeping soundly. Others guests have experienced cold chills when they come within a few yards of what was once her bedroom.

Hotel visitors have often had a wonderful day enjoying the delights of this lovely hotel and after a finishing a good dinner have mounted the creaking stairs of this old manor and climbed into their four-poster bed only to find, to their horror, the shade of the matron hovering in front of them, waiting to make sure that they are well tucked in.

17 The Archer and the Soldier

A horseman's spectre is often seen galloping at full stretch along Shaw Green Lane, which runs east to west through Prestbury not far from the Cheltenham Racecourse.

It is thought that this horseman, a soldier, was heading for Edward IV's camp at Tewkesbury during the War of the Roses when he met his demise. The two dynasties involved in this war were identified by the white rose for York and the red for Lancaster. This war began in 1455 and raged on in sporadic bursts until 1487. The campaign fought under these banners were a series of battles between the two rival houses and the prize was the throne of England. Victory went to the Lancastrian Henry Tudor and subsequently the House of Tudor ruled England and Wales for the next 116 years.

The soldier who was heading for Edward's IV's camp at Tewkesbury never made it, for he was shot through the neck by a very accurate enemy archer just before he turned the corner of Shaw Green Lane to safety. Perhaps the reason this soldier's shade returns again and again is because he was extremely dedicated and feels he must complete his mission. His shade re-enacts this event over and over again and the whole gory scene has been seen and heard on many occasions. This soldier's strangled, gurgling yells when the arrow finds its mark echo along the lane and send chills through all those who witness this ghastly scene. Witnesses say that his horse continues to gallop at full speed as this soldier topples off and lands with a sickening thump. He lies broken and bloody on the ground with the shank of the arrow still sticking out of his neck. His last gasps are heard with tortured clarity and as he finally gives up the struggle he falls back, revealing sightless eyes that stare at the sky. A few seconds later his image disappears. When he returns, the whole scene plays exactly as before and according to witnesses is just as terrifying.

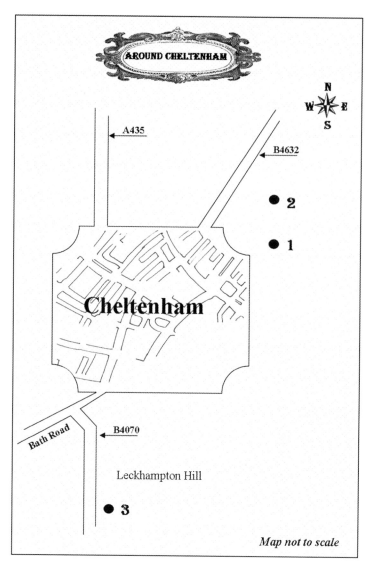

AROUND CHELTENHAM

A435

B4632

● 2

● 1

Cheltenham

Bath Road

B4070

Leckhampton Hill

● 3

Map not to scale

Key to Map

Story	Location	Story Title
1	*Sudeley Castle*	*The Sudeley Castle Shades*
2	*Belas Knap*	*Tumps, Humps and Bumps in the Night*
3	*Leckhampton Hill*	*Devil's Chimney of the Damned*

three

Around Cheltenham

1 The Sudeley Castle Shades

'All you young housemaids will remain chaste while you are working under my governance at Sudeley Castle. Those are the rules and if you break them, you will be dismissed immediately with no pay or references'.

These words were used to admonish the female servants who were hired to work at Sudeley Castle during Victorian times. They were spoken by the head housekeeper, Janet, who, when she was not engaged in her work, lived in a cottage in nearby Rushley Lane. This severe woman wore the typical servant's garb of those times –

Sudeley Castle, steeped in the supernatural.

a high-necked dress, probably made of black bombazine, with a long skirt covered by a starched pinafore. Her hair was neatly tied back and put up in a bun and she wore a white mop cap over it.

Dozens of servants were required to maintain the high standard of living at Sudeley Castle during the Victorian era. Many of the servants under Janet's care were naïve young girls brought over from Wales to fill the positions of scullery maid, kitchen maid, between maid (tweeny), house maid, parlour maid, laundry maid, chamber maid and – the highest of the pecking order – the lady's maid. There were a corresponding number of male servants and Janet was determined to keep them apart. It is thought that she succeeded admirably.

She ruled with an iron hand, nipping in the bud any amorous adventures the young maids might try to have with the male servants also working at the castle. The moment any indiscretions were discovered by Janet, the offender was fired and cast out immediately. She had such a strong hold on her job that she didn't want to leave it – and even though she died, she never did. She haunts Sudeley Castle to this very day, with many sightings of her having been reported over the years.

Sudeley Castle is situated north-east of Cheltenham and is close to Winchcombe, which was once a Saxon town. Sudeley was built in the tenth century and is mentioned in the Domesday Book when it was part of a larger estate in Hawling. There have been numerous owners of this castle over the centuries, including Ethelred the Unready, who maintained

Left: A painting at Sudeley Castle before a ghostly visitor arrives. Right: Could this be the housekeeper's ghost in the same painting?

Ghosts have floated under these arches in Sudeley Castle.

a deer park among the oak trees in the grounds, and King Richard III, who died at the Battle of Bosworth. Elthelred's sister, Goda, inherited the castle from him and as she was related to William of Normandy, Sudeley was spared during the Norman invasion. Goda's descendents continued to live in Sudeley until 1368 when the castle became the property of William Boteler, an admiral in the French wars under both Henry V and Henry VI. Boteler used the wealth he accumulated in the wars to rebuild Sudeley. His additions included Portmere Tower, the tithe barn, the banqueting hall and St Mary's Chapel.

Sudeley Castle was seized in a forced sale by Edward IV after he ascended the throne in 1469 and given to his brother Richard, Duke of Gloucester. Subsequently, the castle was passed on to Edward VI who granted it to his uncle, 1st Baron Thomas Seymour of Sudeley. In 1535 Sudeley Castle was visited by Henry VIII and his second wife, Anne Boleyn. Baron Seymour eventually married the Edward VI's stepmother, Catherine Parr, who had been Henry VIII's sixth wife, and took up residence. Other famous names associated with Sudeley include Lady Jane Grey, who was a ward of Baron Seymour, and also Lady Elizabeth Tudor, daughter of Henry VIII – later Queen Elizabeth I.

Baron Seymour built up Sudeley into a magnificent palace for his new wife, Catherine Parr, but after only two years of marriage she died giving birth to a daughter, Mary. She was buried in the adjoining St Mary's Chapel. A portrait of Catherine Parr and a love letter written to her by Thomas Seymour are on display to visitors of the castle, in addition to the christening robes of Queen Elizabeth I.

In 1592 Sudeley Castle was the scene of an elaborate week-long festivity attended by Queen Elizabeth I to celebrate the anniversary of the defeat of the Spanish Armada, one of three such occasions when she was entertained in the banqueting hall.

During the English Civil War, Lord Chandos of Sudeley supported the Royalists and allowed Prince Rupert, commander of the king's forces, to use Sudeley as a strategic staging point. Subsequently, Sudeley Castle and the chapel were desecrated by Cromwell's men when they stormed it and used it as a garrison headquarters. The Octagon Tower is pitted with marks from the canon fire of the battle. The castle and the entire estate was plundered, ransacked and left an abandoned ruin, and Catherine Parr's grave was not rediscovered until 1728. The roof of Sudeley was removed and many local villagers took stones from the ruins to build homes of their own.

During the first of several Civil War sieges of the castle, Prince Rupert's hunting dog was killed. Almost immediately afterwards the ghost of this dog set about haunting the castle. His pitiful howling has been heard by many occupants over the centuries and he particularly favoured the banqueting hall for his visits from the other side. There are numerous reports of this dog's eerie appearances and he is usually heard panting and snarling before he actually materialises. When he does, he appears suddenly before startled, terrified witnesses and lopes up and down the banqueting hall, apparently

Opposite: *Spooky St Mary's Chapel, in the grounds of the castle.*

The banqueting hall where Prince Rupert's hunting dog lingers.

searching for his master. After several minutes of agitated searching this frustrated, ghostly dog barks loudly and finally disappears with the sound of his yowling still echoing though the castle.

Sudeley Castle lay in ruins for over 200 years before it was purchased in 1837, together with fourteen acres of land, by John and William Dent, who extensively rebuilt the Tudor section of the building. The Dents called in the architect Sir Gilbert Scott to rebuild the chapel and the interior and walls of the castle. When the brothers died, their descendant, Emma Dent, continued the enthusiastic remodelling of the castle and the landscaping of the grounds until her death in 1900. During her restoration of the castle, Lady Dent furnished it with fine paintings and objets d'art, turning it into the very comfortable stately home that it remains to this day. Paintings acquired during this time include works by Rubens, Van Dyck and Turner. There are magnificent stained-glass windows on the staircase of the castle by William Morris, and other treasures include a bed canopy embroidered by Anne Boleyn which adorns the Lace Bedroom, a bed that was specially constructed for a visit by Charles I in the Rupert Room, and a fine display of Civil War artefacts and Jacobean embroidery.

The current owners are Elizabeth, Lady Ashcomber, the wife of Henry Edward Cubitt, 4th Baron Ashcombe, who owns 50 per cent of the castle, and her two children, Henry and Mollie Dent-Brocklehurst, who each own 25 per cent. This curious division of ownership came about because Lady Ashcomber's first husband, Mark Dent-Brocklehurst, died without making a will in 1972.

Sudeley Castle is now open to the public and tours are given of the castle and grounds. It is a splendid sight with its ruins surrounding the inhabited Tudor part of the estate. The gardens boast over 100 different varieties of roses and the Queen's Garden is a copy of the original Tudor parterre. To complete the picture the castle is framed by the halcyon and wooded Cotswold countryside.

Sudeley Castle is also, it seems, a fitting ambience for visitations from the other side and over the years there have been a number of sightings of the aforementioned Janet, the long-dead housekeeper. A witness saw what was thought to be Janet's apparition when she materialised in the needlework room dressed in a house dress, white blouse and mop cap. Her apparition has also been seen leaving the Rupert Room and moving about the main bedroom.

During a recent public tour Janet's ghost chose to make a very dramatic appearance. A tour group had almost completed their viewing of the castle and stood listening to a guide as they gathered at the bottom of a staircase. Among the tourists was a young girl, about the same age as one of the Victorian maids who would have been under Janet's charge. She was standing on a step at the back of this group when she suddenly felt a compelling desire to detach herself from the other tourists and climb the stairs she had just descended. She tried to resist this feeling but finally gave way to it and slipped away

Housekeeper Janet's ghost was seen here in Sudeley Castle.

The ghostly ruins of Portmere Tower, Sudeley Castle.

unnoticed by the other members of the tour. Upon reaching the top of the staircase she was startled to suddenly see, standing in front of a window, the ghost of Janet, who had no doubt returned to admonish her about chastity. Janet was wearing her long Victorian dress and white pinafore and was carrying starched bed linen. She appeared to be going about her duties just as if she were still alive. The young girl who witnessed this was chilled to the bone. She was paralysed with fear as she stared at Janet's eerie, semi-transparent figure for almost a minute before it slowly dissolved and disappeared.

Despite a parade of royal owners and illustrious visitors throughout the centuries, it seems ironic that a servant in the form of the lowly housekeeper and Prince Rupert's hunting dog should be the ghosts who haunt historic Sudeley Castle.

2 Tumps, Humps and Bumps in the Night

Around the year 3000 BC, Neolithic tribes constructed almost eighty massive long barrows in the Cotswold region. These rounded earth humps are thought to be burial mounds and they vary in size. Some of the bigger ones are more than two stories high and extend across several fields. These 'tumps', as they are called by the local inhabitants, do sometimes go bump in the night for they are thought to be haunted by the ghosts of those interred inside.

The Belas Knap long barrow, three miles south of Winchcombe, near Cheltenham, is signposted from a minor road off the A46. This mound is thought to have acquired its name from Baal, a storm god from antiquity. Belas could also be a variation of the Latin word *bellus* meaning 'beautiful' and may be referring to the hill or the view from its summit. Knap is perhaps a variation of 'Cneph', the Egyptian winged symbol, or alternatively Knap could be Old English for 'the crest of a hill'.

The Belas Knap chambered burial mound is over 12ft in height, 178ft long and more than 50ft wide, and the view from the top of the mound reveals magnificent vistas for many miles around. This long barrow has a false entrance that is fronted by a semi-circular forecourt at the northern end and was excavated during Victorian times. Artefacts that were excavated from the long barrow can be seen in the Church Museum at Winchcombe.

In Timothy Darvill's book *Prehistoric Gloucestershire*, he suggests that the H-shaped portal setting of the false entrance represents the remains of an earlier portal dolmen which was later incorporated in the larger tomb. Only the lower courses of drystone walling are original, other additions being modern replacements.

The Victorian excavation revealed four chambers in the burial mound. Two are situated in the north end, one in the south and the last in the long stone cist also at the southern end. During these excavations the skulls of an ancient chieftain and his family, the skeleton of a horse, pottery shards, flint tools and the remains of five children were found when the false entrance was opened up and the original lintel stone removed.

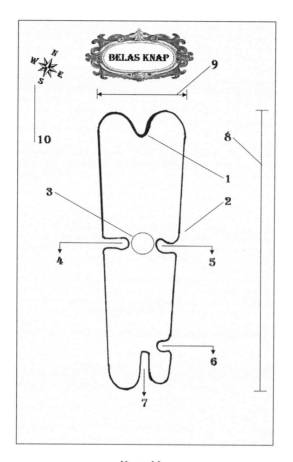

Key to Map

1 False Portal
2 Fallen Lintel
3 Stone Circle
4 North-west Chamber
5 North-east Chamber
6 South-east Chamber
7 South Chamber
8 Length 178ft
9 Width 60ft
10 Mound is 23° west of due north.

The false entrance to Belas Knap long barrow.

The east side of the mound at Belas Knap long barrow.

West entrance of Belas Knap, where sprites frolic.

The roofs of these chambers are modern reconstructions which were erected during restoration in the early 1930s. More recently, excavators discovered the remains of about forty people who were probably buried at various times over the centuries and most likely do not date from the time of the original construction of the mound.

It is suggested that serious ghost hunters visit the Belas Knap long barrow either at the time of the solstice or at night, although perhaps this recommendation is only for the hardy because scaling the top of the mound requires a two mile uphill walk. The great mound of earth that was laboriously built so long ago must have needed incredible numbers of labourers to erect. When the long barrow is visited at night it looms up against the moon and on stormy evenings the wind screams around it, as if warning those who are alive that the undead are about to slip out of their eerie chambers deep inside and haunt all those who dare to venture close.

Strange manifestations have been documented on numerous occasions with regards to this burial mound. Weird vibrations of the earth have been felt by witnesses either standing in or on the mound. These vibrations were said to resemble severe seismic activity although no earthquakes were reported at the time. They are said to be unique to this site and those who have experienced them say that the initial movement seems to come from inside the mound and gradually enters the body of everybody standing nearby. On one occasion several witnesses reported that when they visited the site during a solstice a paralysis overcame them followed by a painful attack of pins and needles.

Within a few minutes a new sensation racked their bodies; it was a trembling, humming vibration that started in their extremities and gradually worked its way into the core of all those present. This was followed by a strange feeling of being at one with, and part of, the burial mound. Visitors to the site who experience these vibrations enter a trance-like state, as if hypnotised. Usually the vibrations stop after a period of time that ranges from ten minutes to half an hour, although the trance-like state does not dissipate for several more hours, or for some days in the case of 'sensitives'.

One visitor was climbing the mound when she noticed a group of monks slowly making their way across a field in the distance. She quickly descended in order to investigate but when she reached ground level the terrain suddenly looked completely different, even though she was looking at the same field. Eventually, she realised that she must have slipped into another dimension or momentarily looked through a tear in the time-space continuum, because the landscape she viewed from near the top of the mound had been that of another time. When she studied old engravings of the area and found paintings of monks wearing similar habits she realised that somehow she had been transported back to medieval times and had been viewing a scene that was at least 500 years old.

Another manifestation seen in and around the burial mound consists of glowing orbs of light that appear suddenly with no prior warning. These orbs become bigger or smaller depending on the time of year and the advent of the solstice. The orbs, generally white in colour, have been known to shine so brightly that they temporarily

The view from Belas Knap, where centuries pass in minutes.

Belas Knap at night.

blind any witnesses who stare into their depths. Also, those who are present when the orbs manifest are often left with an uneasy feeling for a very long time afterwards. This feeling of unexplained dread has been known to cause terrible despair, especially to those who are of a more sensitive nature. Sometimes these feelings are so extreme and persistent that an exorcism finally becomes necessary.

In addition, the witnesses who have stared at the orbs have had nightmares involving ancient ghosts that appeared as howling skeletons, fantastic slime-ridden creatures or knife-wielding maniacs who slash at these poor souls until most of them are startled awake, screaming in fear. Those who endure these nightmares also recount images of weird flashing orbs and terrifying feelings of the earth moving underfoot. In these dreams massive fissures rend the earth and volcanic craters appear, spewing fire, huge rocks and smoke. Boiling lava then cascades all over the earth before the entire image transmogrifies into a horrific line-up of evil ghosts with the scariest visages ever seen. One victim of this manifestation deliberately induced insomnia with many cups of coffee and other stimulants because of his fear of experiencing another

Looking out of the east entrance of Belas Knap.

traumatic nightmare. However, this was found to be no solution as after excessive sleep deprivation hallucinations set in and this victim was no better off than before. All the witnesses who have experienced this particular manifestation declared that they had no wish to revisit this burial mound ever again.

Some of the ghosts who haunt Belas Knap are said to be very festive and the sounds of their party-making has been heard by many people over the centuries. Witnesses have described the voices that have emanated from this long barrow as sounding like large crowds of people having a very noisy late-night party. These voices are usually giggling, laughing, talking and calling out to one another. It seems that the otherworldly inhabitants of these long barrows are a range of: goblins, which are ugly, evil grotesques; hobgoblins, known as mischievous, puckish spirits; and sprites, which are best described as elf-like ghosts.

The ghost hunter, however, should heed the warning that the celebratory antics of these goblins, hobgoblins and sprites can be a tragic trap. The sound of the party-making is deceptively friendly and welcoming, but in fact it serves as an evil lure. For legend has it that anybody made of human flesh and blood who is tempted to enter the long barrow and join in the revelry for the night will be taking a great risk. It is said that all who climb into the long barrow and eat or drink any offerings from the goblins and sprites inside will never be seen again.

Even if the temptation to accept any offerings is overcome, if the unwary ghost hunter still spends time with these evil poltergeists he or she could find that, upon returning to the outside world, dozens of years have gone by as all those who entered the long barrow are now living in another era.

Surely there could be no greater horror than that of the young woman who, as legend has it, entered one of these evil chambers as a young, pretty, smooth-faced girl and then, seemingly after mere moments had passed, returned to the sunlight to see in a mirror the face of an ancient, ugly crone with missing, broken teeth, wispy grey hair and a thousand wrinkles.

3 Devil's Chimney of the Damned

Leckhampton Hill is thought to be an evil place, especially at night when thunder rolls and lightning flashes across its ancient terrain. One account from long ago tells of a man climbing up Leckhampton Hill in the dead of night in a terrible hailstorm and, despite the racket of the storm, suddenly hearing rattling chains.

The deafening noise of these chains clanked eerily and seemed to come from everywhere at once. This poor man clasped his hands to his ears, desperate to lessen the sound, but the scraping of metal against metal still filled his head. He dashed in every direction to escape, but the sound of the chains stayed with him no matter how fast he ran. Next he saw a low outcrop of rock ahead of him and jumped over it, thinking to crouch down and shelter from the terrible noise. The moment that he vaulted the rocks he saw, to his horror, a burning inferno beneath him. He managed to land on a small ledge which stopped him from falling into the fiery depths below. He clung precariously to the rocks as his narrow perch gradually crumbled away under his feet. The bottomless fiery chasm below him continuously spewed ash and flaming rocks which narrowly missed him as they flew past his head. At one point he almost fell headlong into the red-hot pit as he dodged them. His efforts caused him to almost lose his footing on more than one occasion and he despaired of getting out of this situation alive. As he struggled, he became aware of an entity next to him on the ledge. This shadowy figure tried to push him into the fire below and he felt an invisible hand pressing him forward. He screamed in terror, which only caused the entity to redouble its efforts. It was only when this brave man prayed out loud that the entity faded slowly away. It is no surprise that all this happened right at the Devil's Chimney.

Opposite: *Is the Devil's Chimney a portal to Hell?*

The famous landmark of the Devil's Chimney on the upper incline of Leckhampton Hill is an amazing sight. This limestone rock formation towers over an abandoned quarry near the top of the hill. It gained its name from its fantastic, twisted shapes which are reminiscent of a crazily shaped chimney, and it is thought to have been constructed by quarrymen in the eighteenth century. It overlooks Cheltenham and the far-distant rolling Cotswold Hills affording spectacular views for miles around. The summit is 925ft above sea level and the hill covers 245 acres of limestone grassland. Old tramway lines still cross the hill from the days of limestone quarrying and the remains of various kilns and quarry workings are dotted about. The stone that was mined from these quarries was used to construct many of the buildings in Cheltenham. This area has been declared a site of Special Scientific Interest because of the surrounding calcareous grassland and the hill's geological significance.

Local legend suggests that the Devil lives beneath the ground on which this chimney sits. Apparently the many Christian churches in the nearby villages enrage the Devil and on Sundays he emerges from his pit, sits on top of Leckhampton Hill and rains rocks down on parishioners in Leckhampton village lying below.

This village, situated on the southern edge of Cheltenham, was in existence during Saxon times and the remains of a moat have been found from that era on Church Farm. In the eighth century this village was the home farm of the royal manor of Cheltenham and was later recorded in the Domesday Book in 1086 under the name Lechametone. This roughly translates to 'the dwelling where garlic or leeks are grown'. The old part of the village was built around the fourteenth-century Church of St Peter on Church Road, and it was said to be the churchgoers from this parish in particular who endured the Devil's attacks.

This church was constructed by Sir John Giffard, the lord of the manor at Leckhampton in the fourteenth century. Sir John also built Leckhampton Court, which is described in Nicholas Kingsley's book *Country Houses of Gloucestershire* as 'one of the grandest medieval houses in Gloucestershire'. The court is situated on a spring which was most likely the reason this site was chosen by the original builders. The water for this dwelling was stored in an underground reservoir in one corner of the kitchen garden. In the fifteenth century new wings were built to the north and the south and the exterior architecture of the south wing has remained largely unchanged since that time. Unfortunately, a large part of the north wing burned down in 1732 due to a fire caused by an abandoned bowl of charcoal.

In 1894, at the Plough Inn Hotel in Cheltenham High Street, Leckhampton Court was sold at auction to John Hargreaves, who had been a tenant there since 1872. The court was passed on to his daughter, Muriel, when he died and she married Cecil Elwes of Colesbourne Park. Today the agricultural land surrounding Leckhampton Court is administered by the Elwes Trust.

The court was used by the British Red Cross during the First World War as a hospital for wounded soldiers. It was requisitioned by the War Office during the Second World

Eerie Devil's Chimney on Leckhampton Hill.

War and became the home of the Durham Light Infantry. When the Americans arrived at Leckhampton Court in 1942, the American film star Mickey Rooney was briefly billeted there.

In 1969 Leckhampton Court was sold to the Sue Ryder Foundation and in 1986 Prince Charles agreed to be the patron of Leckhampton Court Care Centre.

Sir John Giffard ensured he would not be forgotten, for not only did he build Leckhampton Court but his tomb and life-sized effigy can been seen in a corner of St Peter's Church to this day. Two figures carved of stone representing Sir John, who died in 1330, and his wife lie on pillows supported by angels, while their feet are held up by a lion and a dog. These carvings are thought to be the finest examples in the entire country constructed during this period.

The medieval Church of St Peter's, with its slender spire and elegant proportions, is thought to have been built on the site of an earlier church because there is documentation of a priest having been fined 2s for non-payment of dues to the canons of Cirencester Abbey by Archbishop Thomas Becket. The church has a ring of eight bells and in the churchyard there is a memorial to Dr Edward Wilson who was lost on Scott's last Antarctic expedition.

Perhaps it is just as well that Leckhampton's name means 'the place where garlic is grown', because this pungent plant has traditionally been used to ward off the Devil.

Or maybe it was the Christian churches of the area that prevailed against Satan as the stones that were hurled down on the villagers were apparently turned back and forced him below ground, where he became trapped and unable to continue this evil practice. Supposedly the stones that the Devil amassed were used by him to build the chimney through which the smoke from the fires of Hell were released.

Villagers were said to leave money on top of the chimney as a bribe to stop the Devil's evil doings. In exchange, the Devil was expected to stay in his underground dwelling and leave these people in peace.

In contrast to these occult theories, David Bick suggests in his book *Old Leckhampton* that the Devil's Chimney was not in fact built by quarrymen or the Devil, but was constructed to publicise Cheltenham in its early days as a spa town. This account would seem to tie in with the landmark's name first appearing in print in 1803.

The nineteenth-century geologist S. Buckman offered a different theory. He maintained that the Devil's Chimney is the result of erosion whittling away a hard column of rock. He stated that soft rock surrounding this column has been worn away over time to reveal the interesting shapes that remain.

The chimney was damaged by an earthquake in 1926 when several cracks appeared. It was repaired in 1985 and made safe from previous erosion. In the past as many as a dozen people are said to have climbed to the top of the chimney at one time, although now it is fenced off for safety.

The Devil's Chimney can be reached via the A46 southbound out of Cheltenham, then onto the B4070 through Leckhampton. Turn left near the peak of the hill onto Hartley Lane, along which is a car park.

Access to the Devil's Chimney is reached by two extremely steep footpaths, one from Daisy Road and the other from Hartley Lane. A viewpoint provides an excellent position for visitors and photographers to appreciate this landmark's silhouette in the late hours of the day, especially during winter months.

The poor beleaguered man who found himself at the Devil's Chimney that terrifying night had further agonies to endure. After the entity who tried to push him off his ledge disappeared, a fusillade of rocks rained down upon him. This man crouched down and held his hands over his head and barely survived the onslaught. When the rocks stopped falling he felt a strange compulsion to stare down into the molten, fiery sea below him. He became mesmerised by the heat and intensity of what he saw. Suddenly, he realised that he was looking straight through the gates of Hell itself. He knew that unless he drew his eyes away from this horrific sight all would be lost, for he was experiencing a terrible desire to step off his ledge into the burning pit. With a superhuman burst of willpower he looked away and then spotted a path through the rocks that had previously remained hidden. He dashed through it to freedom. When he told his story many people begged to be led back to the exact spot of this terrible experience, but nothing would induce this terrified man to return to the horrors of the Devil's Chimney on Leckhampton Hill.

Sources

Books

Adby-Collins, B., *The Morton Ghost*
Bardens, D., *Ghosts and Hauntings* (Ace Press, 1969)
Brooks, J. A., *Ghosts and Witches of the Cotswolds* (Jarrold, Norwich, 1981)
Devereux, P., *Haunted Land* (Piatkus Books, 2003)
Palmer, Roy, *The Folklore of Gloucestershire* (Westcountry Books, 1994)
The Reader's Digest Association Ltd, Folklore, *Myths and Legends of Britain* (1973)
Scarre, Chris, *The Megalithic Monuments of Great Britain and Ireland* (J.M. Dent, 2005)
Service, A. & Bradbery, J., *The Standing Stones of Europe* (J. M. Dent, 1993)
Titchmarsh, Peter, *The Cotswolds Town and Village Guide* (Reardon Publishing, 2000)

Websites

archenfield.com
bbc.co.uk/gloucestershire
borleyrectorycompanion.co.uk
britainexpress.com
british-history.ac.uk
cheltenham4u.co.uk
cheltenham.blogspot.com
cheltenhamtownhall.org.uk
everymantheatre.org.uk
forteantimes,com
geocities.com
theheritagetrail.co.uk
independent.co.uk/sport/general/
locutus.ucr.edu
paranormaldatabase.com/
gloucestershire/glosdata.php
parkfarmcolwall.co.uk/history/
MedievalHistory.php
pauldevereux.co.uk.
sudeleycastle.co.uk
telegraph.co.uk/culture/books
timeshighereducation.co.uk.
worcestercitymuseums.org.uk

Other titles published by The History Press

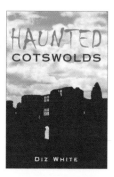

Haunted Cotswolds

DIZ WHITE

Spine-chilling tales of ghosts, ghouls and the undead have been gathered here from every corner of the Cotswolds, revealing in heart-stopping detail this region's unexplained events and the creepy elements that lurk just beneath its rolling hills and beautiful vistas. Descriptions of Cotswold architecture and history are woven into thrilling stories of supernatural happenings, promising those with an interest in the paranormal terrifying dreams for years to come.

978 0 7524 5426 9

Georgian Cheltenham

EDITH HUMPHRIS & CAPTAIN E.C. WILLOUGHBY

As a spa town, Georgian Cheltenham was visited by thousands seeking the solace of its healing waters, but as a pleasure resort it attracted distinguished and/or fashionable people of the day. This book focuses on the late eighteenth and early nineteenth centuries, beginning with the visit of King George in 1788, which really brought it to prominence.

978 1 8458 8606 6

Haunted Gloucester

EILEEN FRY & ROSEMARY HARVEY

Gloucester's historic docks have some strange stories to tell and the city's twelfth-century cathedral also has its secrets. From a ghostly procession at Berkeley Castle to the Grey Lady at the old Theatre Royal, this new and fascinating collection of strange sightings and happenings in the city's streets, churches and public houses is sure to appeal to anyone intrigued by Gloucester's haunted heritage.

978 0 7524 3312 7

A Grim Almanac of Gloucestershire

ROBIN BROOKS

Gloucestershire is especially good at blending the quaint with the brutal. Where else could you find a village that celebrates Pig Face Day once a year – and guess what's on the menu? There is much between these covers that will make you raise an eyebrow, curl a toe and cross your legs. Prepare for your stomach to be turned, your brow to be furrowed and your funny bones to be tickled by these true tales of grim Gloucestershire.

978 0 7524 5679 9

Visit our website and discover thousands of other History Press books.

www.thehistorypress.co.uk